*Swami Vivekananda*

# Relief of
# Tension, Depression
# & Anxiety through
# SPIRITUAL LIVING

## SWAMI TATHAGATANANDA

It is a change of the soul itself for the better that alone
will cure the evils of life. No amount of force, or government, or legislative cruelty will change the conditions of
a race, but it is spiritual culture and ethical culture alone
that can change wrong . . . tendencies for the better.

—Swami Vivekananda, *Complete Works*, III: 182

## Advaita Ashrama
(Publication Department)
5 Dehi Entally Road
Kolkata 700 014

*Published by*
Swami Bodhasarananda
President, Advaita Ashrama
Mayawat, Champawat, Uttaranchal
*through its Publication Department, Kolkata*
Web-site: *www.advaitaashrama.org*
E-mail: *mail@advaitaashrama.org*

ISBN 81-7505-298-8

Those who wish to learn in greater detail about the
teachings contained in this book may write to:
Spiritual Leader, Vedanta Society of
New York, 34 West 71st Street,
New York, NY 10023, U.S.A.

*Printed in India at*
Trio Process
Kolkata 700 014

This book
is
dedicated
to
**Surya Narayana—The Sun-God**
(Chandogya Upanishad, 3.19.1)
With loving devotion
and humble salutations.

*"The sun is the great mother. All life on earth might be considered as transient materialization of the exhaustless floods of radiance which she pours on the planet's surface. This enables green plants to synthesize sugars and starches from water in the soil and from carbon dioxide gas in the atmosphere, thus making possible the emergence of all other forms of life on earth by producing the essential foods. We eat sunshine in sugar, bread, and meat, burn sunshine of millions of years ago in coal and oil, wear sunshine in wool and cotton. Sunshine makes the wind and the rain, the summers and winters of years and of ages. Inextricably interwoven are the threads of life and light."*

**— Thomas R. Henry —**
in his article, 'The Smithsonian Institution',
*The National Geographic Magazine*, September 1948.

# PUBLISHER'S NOTE

We take great pleasure in presenting this book, *Relief of Tension, Depression and Anxiety through Spiritual Living*, as we believe the practical suggestions given by its author will do much to relieve people of the tensions of modern life. This work is meant not only for those expressly suffering from mental tensions, but also for all of us who are swept up in this fast-paced, high-tech world that is devoid of any concern for human feelings.

There has long been a need for a work that establishes the all-round benefits of spiritual living, and this book fills that gap. It is like a beacon light that directs itself to all corners of the mind, dispelling all our fears and anxieties. It shows how spiritual values alone can bring peace and integrity to our life, and how a society bereft of spirituality will necessarily give rise to more asylums and correctional institutions. Even while dealing with modern struggles, the learned author has upheld traditional values.

We are grateful to all those who have helped us in the publication of this volume. We shall consider our endeavour amply rewarded if our readers benefit from this book and send us feedback about its influence on their lives.

Kolkata                                       PUBLISHER
January 12, 2008

# CONTENTS

## 1

## SOME BASIC PRINCIPLES
## OF SPIRITUAL LIVING

## 2

## THE BROAD QUESTION OF CULTURE AND CIVILIZATION

CONTENTS

# 3

## THE GREATEST MEDICAL
## PROBLEM OF THE CENTURY

# 4

## PRACTICAL SPIRITUAL PRINCIPLES
## TO ALLEVIATE STRESS

# CONCLUSION

# THE DEEPER SIGNIFICANCE
# OF SPIRITUAL LIFE

# PREFACE

As the source of all things, life is divine through and through. Therefore, our fundamental problems in life can only be solved when we are able to discover the centre of life, which is our hidden divinity. Though the subject-matter appears diverse, the unity of thought and projection of the image of divinity upon every topic in this humble work will not escape the notice of a perceptive reader.

Many of the topics are important to spiritual seekers no matter what path they have chosen. Generally, they all direct the reader to a scheme of holistic living instead of a modern lifestyle bereft of spiritual insights. Society currently faces the problems raised by a critical erosion of positive, life-building and life-sustaining values. Lacking exposure to "sane values," moderns are typically irreverent and casual about deeper philosophical questions that more thoughtful people contemplate.

If one's objective is a sincere pursuit of all-round well-being through a healthy scheme of life, a holistic, integrated, stable life of righteousness can be actualized. This remains true in diverse circumstances. My own modest objective in responding to the urgent, apparent need for a holistic view of life is an earnest hope that this humble work may evoke interest in that direction.

I am indebted to Renu Pandita of Columbia University for supplying me with numerous volumes and Shakuntala Sarkar, PhD, for providing many extracts pertinent to this book. Mrs. Probhati Mukherjee of New Delhi and Professor

Joanne Kilgour Dowdy went through the entire manuscript in its preliminary stage. I thank them for their kind help.

If the reader is benefited in any way by reading this book, I shall consider their benefit to be the fruit of my labour of love.

*Om Sri Ramakrishnarpanam astu!*

July 10, 2007                    Swami Tathagatananda

The Vedanta Society of New York
34 West 71st Street
New York, NY 10023

# FOREWORD

We are obsessed with our bodies and generally with the material aspects of life, to the detriment of our souls and the spiritual dimension of life. As Swami Tathagatananda explains in his book, this is the main cause of the epidemic of tension, anxiety, depression, fear, gloom and insecurity in our time. When these are in the mind they have a negative effect on our physical health. The root cause of these problems is the lack of a spiritual dimension in our lives. Organic foods, over-the-counter pills, psychotropic medications and hallucinogenic drugs will not cure our emotional ailments. From the first line of his book to the last, Swami Tathagatananda explains that effective relief from the psychological problems that beset us can only come from changing the emphasis in our lives from the worldly and selfish to the spiritual and unselfish. He does this in various ways and from many angles.

In the course of his book Swami Tathagatananda draws some significant distinctions, which at first glance, might seem surprising. The first is to differentiate culture from civilization. They are related but not the same. Civilization is compared to the body and culture to the soul. Civilization has to do with the external, the material, the mastery of nature and worldly life. Culture, "the domain of values," is concerned with the internal, the moral and depends on eternal spiritual values: "Great civilizations possess utilitarian knowledge, civic services and material pleasures that bring worldly happiness to society; great cultures contribute to a refined humanity that enjoys vertical spiritual growth." Only a spiritual life can bring lasting peace and joy in life. Culture involves the elevation and implementation of spiritual values. Culture helps us to overcome egoism by leading us to recognize our spiritual connection with the Divine. "Unity with the Divine fulfills the one desire that underlies all the other desires that hide it from our view. Our need is for unity with the all-loving Divine." Without this, we always feel a lack in our lives, as St. Augustine explains so well in his *Confessions*. With unity in the Divine, we have everything.

Another important distinction is presented in the book: "There is an essential distinction between "fun" and "joy." Fun or amusement is temporary and "tends to lead us away from morality and virtue," whereas lasting, profound joy comes from spiritual living and self-control. In his well-known book, *Amusing Ourselves to Death*, sociologist Neil Postman carefully explains that the quest for amusement has become a sort of religion in the West, especially in America. The quest for fun has permeated our society, invading not just family life and friendships but also education, work and even religious teaching. There is a place for just about everything in the modern world but when frivolity takes over a society, that society is characterized by superficial goals and dissatisfaction in life. The struggle to have fun in life is a superficial struggle that brings no lasting joy, in spite of all our efforts. Joyfulness arises from the inner harmony that can only come from living a moral and spiritual life. This inner and outer joyfulness is the value of cheerfulness.

Cheerfulness not only contributes to mental and physical health, it reflects a spiritual orientation in life. We need only think of the Elder Zossima in Dostoevsky's *The Brothers Karamazov* to understand this point. Though suffering from a mortal illness, Zossima, greeted everyone with cheerfulness, uplifting all who came to see him with their problems. His steadfast, cheerful attitude was the result of his spiritual attainment. Dostoevsky based this character on a real person of his acquaintance.

Swami Tathagatananda also distinguishes spiritual solitude from the various sorts of ordinary human loneliness. "Man is solitary by choice; his strength of mind depends on inner soul awareness. . . . Religion is what we do in our solitariness." On the other hand, "Man is lonely by indifference and neglect; through weakness of mind he depends on external, impermanent and material things."

Swami Tathagatananda gives the basic message of unity with the Divine in wave after wave of material which has the cumulative effect of pushing us away from aimless, sensate life and into spiritual life. He helps us to overcome our "spiritual lethargy" so that we can substitute an uplifted, unselfish mind for a "mind soaked in materialism." "Spiritual life minimizes stress through the effective control of the mind," severing the root of our emotional problems. Through spiritual practices we can replace negative emotions, instead of wallowing in them. Instead of giving in to our current love affair with the freedom to do anything, which enslaves us to harmful habits, the Swami urges us to develop "a pure mind which is an infinite storehouse of power" and gives us a prescription for doing so.

March 28, 2007                    Samuel D. Fohr
                                  Professor of Philosophy
                                  University of Pittsburgh

# INTRODUCTION

The Age of Progress and Science in which we currently live is also variously described as the Age of Tension, the Age of Anxiety, the Age of Depression, the Age of Violence, the Age of Crime, the Age of Fear. Reflecting on this, we find that evil essentially stems from ignorance of the spiritual dimension of life. Swami Vivekananda says, "It is a change of the soul itself for the better that alone will cure the evils of life. No amount of force, or government, or legislative cruelty will change the conditions of a race, but it is spiritual culture and ethical culture alone that can change wrong . . . tendencies for the better" (*C. W.*, III: 182).

Secular knowledge does not give us Self-knowledge. Though it gives us miraculous control over Nature, worldly knowledge does very little to help us control our emotions and social behaviour. As a result, our life is oriented to external objects. We have every sort of possession except self-possession. We are obsessed with physical security but lack emotional and spiritual security. Spiritual knowledge encourages values that motivate us to improve our human worth. Spiritual insight harmonizes and enriches our subjective life. It helps us acquire positive, enduring values to live by.

Everything has improved in our nuclear age except our values of life. Most of us associate "value" with "pay, promotion and pleasure." We do not feel we have to account for any lack of integrity in these pursuits. The tense, insecure and fearful mood that prevails in a world of increased violence and terrorism separates us from our spiritual foundation of life. A pall of existential gloom envelops us, making us psychically and physically weak:

> Man suffers intellectually from a sense of insecurity, ethically from a sense of anxiety. In moments of self-analysis, he examines his past and feels distressed in spirit, unsure of himself, pulled this way and that. He becomes embittered, sick unto death. He is haunted with a sense of mystery, has the feeling of being weak, incompetent, frail, ignorant, evil, unholy. This unhappy being, whose heart is torn by secret sufferings, is terribly alone, struggling not with external forces but with himself. This divided, riven being, tormented by fear, at odds with himself, is weighed down by despair. There is no unhappiness greater than that of division. (S. Radhakrishnan, *Recovery of Faith* (1955), p. 98)

The time has arrived for us to make more practical use of our moral and spiritual insights and to pursue "right conduct" with greater enthusiasm. We are to surrender outdated attitudes and incorporate a new vision of human progress that is based on spiritual growth.

Hungarian chemist Albert Szent-Györgi received the Nobel Prize (1937) for his discovery of Vitamin C. He said, "Snakes can grow only by bursting their skins. Molting has to be a painful process and should it fail, the snake would die. Mankind grows by bursting the outgrown skin of antiquated ideas, thinking, and institutions." Our thick-skinned superficial ideas must be sloughed off if we are to survive.

The dimension of our inner mind is shrunken and frail from lack of spiritual nourishment; our outer life is bloated with over indulgence. Our meaningless secular lifestyles and single-minded material pursuits reflect a shallow spiritual dimension of life. Progress signifies more than speed and comfort; it indicates direction and purpose that culminate in self-fulfilment.

Plainly, human progress has no meaning without awakened, active spiritual values. Life is significant precisely because of the capacity we have to strive for the imperative ideals considered vital over the long ages. Sages and saints have treasured this pursuit above all others for the purity, strength and nobility it imparts. The same ideals improve the lives of ordinary men and women and give the gift of a strengthened, resolute mind guided by a noble outlook.

A worthy life is one that absorbs and implements the conveyed wisdom and honoured traditions of our long human heritage. Information does not constitute knowledge, nor does knowledge constitute wisdom. If personality is to be transformed, knowledge must attain to wisdom. "Unless men increase in wisdom as much as in knowledge, increase in knowledge will be increase in sorrow" (Bertrand Russell, *Impact of Science on Society*, pp. 120-1).

Values emerge at all levels in society. A true community maintains itself and harmonizes its practical and spiritual goals by cultivating the fundamental virtues of renunciation and service that produce humane, cultured, unselfish citizens. To foster a spiritual attitude and generate ethical and moral culture are the chief objectives of society.

Our ideas determine our views. Our conception of life sets the entire tone of our way of life. We can trace all conflict of ideas and world views to the mental constitution and cultural background of individuals. The wrong conception of life is the root of conflict in the world, wherein the price of ignorance is heavy. All our troubles are due to spiritual ignorance.

We are the focus of all values. India's mystics delving deep into the self had the revelation of an infinite vista of human potential. We are the epitome of the cosmos. In Swami

Vivekananda's words, "Man is the most representative being in the universe, the microcosm, a small universe in himself" (*C. W.*, IV: 49).

Vedanta's central theme is monism—the individual and the Supreme Self are one in their essential nature. Man is divine. "Self" in Vedanta is Self-luminous, eternally pure and blissful. Because it is not a created entity, it is immutable, eternal, immortal and infinite. This Soul within us is the only source of all virtues, joy, peace, wisdom, power and knowledge. Self-knowledge is the crowning glory of life. Ignorant of the Self, we live in bondage and suffering.

"In man, things which are not measurable are more important than those which are measurable" (Dr. Alexis Carrel in *Man, the Unknown*). Value-oriented culture attaches maximum importance to unfolding the Soul-force through the spiritual disciplines of self-control and morality. Right living requires right understanding. Whether our inclination is spiritual or secular, we cannot neglect the moral virtues. The *Bhagavad Gita* (XVI: 1) enumerates them. Truthfulness, self-control, uprightness, purity, renunciation, patience, selflessness are generally known as the fruits of the soul. They equip us for the experience of peace, harmony and fulfilment. In trial and tribulation, they give us stability and inspiration to wage the battle of life. They give us self-confidence and fearlessness. Mere intellectual growth unaccompanied by the fruits of the soul produces egoism, aggression and many other human weaknesses in us. "Unless above himself he erects himself, how poor a thing is man" (William Wordsworth).

Our need of spiritual enlightenment is pragmatic. Arnold Toynbee points out: "In these circumstances, it might be forecast that, in the next chapter of the world's history, mankind would seek compensation for the loss of much of its political, economic and perhaps even domestic freedom by putting more of its treasure into spiritual freedom . . . ." (*A Historian's Approach to Religion*, p. 244). He goes on to say, "In a regimented world, the realm of the spirit may be freedom's citadel" (Ibid., p. 249). Toynbee exhorts us to re-orient ourselves spiritually in the atomic age:

> The time has come for us, in our turn, to wrench ourselves out of the seventeenth-century mathematico-physical line of approach which we are still following, and to make a fresh start from the spiritual side. This is now, once again, the more promising approach of the two if we are right in expecting that, in the atomic age which opened in AD 1945, the spiritual field of activity, not the physical one, is going to be the domain of freedom." (Ibid., pp. 286-7)

# 1

# SOME BASIC PRINCIPLES
# OF SPIRITUAL LIVING

## HUMAN LIFE IS A UNION OF SOUL
## AND NATURE, OF SPIRIT AND MATTER

*Do you know how much energy, how many powers,
how many forces are still lurking behind that frame of
yours? What scientist has known all that is in man?
Millions of years have passed since man first came here,
and yet but one infinitesimal part of his powers has been
manifested. Therefore, you must not say that you are
weak. How do you know what possibilities lie behind
that degradation on the surface? You know but little of
that which is within you. For behind you is the ocean of
infinite power and blessedness....*

*Fill yourselves with the ideal; whatever you do, think
well on it. All your actions will be magnified,
transformed, deified, by the very power of the thought. If
matter is powerful, thought is omnipotent. Bring this
thought to bear upon your life, fill yourselves with the
thought of your almightiness, your majesty, and your
glory.*

—Swami Vivekananda,
*Complete Works, II: 301-3 passim*

Our conception of life is very important. The entire
direction of our life depends on it. Spiritual life begins with

the wisdom that Pure Consciousness, or Supreme Self, or Soul, is behind our intellect, mind, ego and body. Of these, the Soul is the true essence behind man's complex nature. Therefore, the real nature of man's mind is spiritual. As the moon reflects the borrowed light of the sun, the light of the Soul animates the mind and the different organs. Sri Ramakrishna says:

> The milk in the pot hisses and swells as long as there is heat under it. Take away the heat, the milk will quiet down as before. (Swami Nikhilananda, trans. *The Gospel of Sri Ramakrishna* [New York: Ramakrishna-Vivekananda Center, 1992], p. 668)

Human life is a union of spirit and matter, a unity of many dimensions—freedom and bondage, purity and impurity, wisdom and ignorance, strength and weakness. This vast and varied universe is the projection of God, the only Reality behind the universe. The divine essence animates the body, mind, etc. Sri Shankara's *Hymn to Dakshinamurti* brings out the idea that the Self functions through the mind, sense organs and body:

> Just as the rays of the light hidden in a pot with a number of holes emanate through those holes, the Self manifests itself through the eyes and sense organs giving rise to the notion "I know." Every object shines (i.e., is known) after the Self manifests it. I bow down to that teacher who is known as Dakshinamurti, who is none other than the Supreme Self.

The Bible says, "I am the vine, ye are the branches: He that abideth in me, and I in him, the same bringeth forth much fruit: for without me ye can do nothing" (John 15: 5). It says again, "That was the true light, which lighteth every man that cometh into the world" (John: 1: 9) and refers to the greatest prevailing human ignorance: "In him was life; and the life was the light of men. And the light shineth in darkness; and the darkness comprehendeth it not" (John: 1: 4-5).

Ignorance of our own divinity impels us to identify with the body, mind and ego. This is the root of all our troubles. The worldliness that tempts our lower mind with base suggestions constantly deceives us. In the words of Jesus: "Whatsoever entereth in at the mouth goeth into the belly and is cast out into the draught. But those things which proceed out of the mouth come forth from the heart; and they defile the man. For out of the heart proceed evil thoughts, murders, adulteries, fornications, thefts, false witness, and blasphemies. These are the things which defile a man" (Matthew, xv: 18-20).

We are burdened with the heavy baggage of unspiritual worldly thoughts that upset our innate balance. Plato says, "Make the boat light by throwing the cargo overboard." When a boat moving across the sea is about to sink, its captain apprehends the danger. He has the moral right to lighten the ship by unloading the baggage in order to save the more precious lives of the passengers. With the same decisiveness, we must reject unspiritual thoughts as a threat to our life and happiness. Swami Vivekananda says:

According to Yoga philosophy, it is through ignorance that the soul has been joined with nature. The aim is to get rid of nature's control over us. That is the goal of all religions. Each soul is potentially divine. The goal is to manifest this Divinity within, by controlling nature, external and internal. Do this either by work, or worship, or psychic control, or philosophy—by one or more or all of these— and be free. This is the whole of religion. Doctrines, or dogmas, or rituals, or books, or temples, or forms, are but secondary details. The Yogi tries to reach this goal through psychic control. Until we can free ourselves from nature, we are slaves; as she dictates so we must go. (*C. W.*, I: 257)

The depth-dimension in every human being is *Atman*, the Self or Soul. Knowledge of our divinity inspires our identification with the *Atman*. This knowledge is the essence of spiritual culture. Swamiji says, "Faith in God and in one's own Self is virtue; doubt is sin. The different scriptures only show the means of attaining virtue" (*C. W.*, V: 419).

No religion tells us, "Be bad and do evil." To the contrary, all religions say, "Do good and be good." The true seeker is a mature person. Gordon Allport writes that seeking religion with higher understanding and higher values constitutes "mature religion." Vedanta's purposeful ethical and moral teachings guide us to the understanding that we are established in universal consciousness as integrated personalities. Everything else we believe is founded on this conviction:

> . . . what a man believes to a large extent determines his mental and physical health. What he believes about his business, his associates, his wife, his immediate future, is important; even more so, what he believes about life in general, its purpose and design. Religious belief, simply because it deals with fundamentals, often turns out to be the most important belief of all. (Gordon W. Allport, *The Individual and His Religion* [New York, 1950], p. 70)

For analytical psychologist and philosopher Carl Jung, ". . . the idea of an all-powerful divine Being is present everywhere, unconsciously if not consciously, because it is an archetype . . . I, therefore, consider it wiser to acknowledge the idea of God consciously" (*Collected Works of C. G. Jung,* Vol. I, p. 70). He wrote, ". . . the ego is ill for the very reason that it is cut off from the whole and has lost its connection with mankind as well as with the Spirit" (Carl G. Jung, *Modern Man in Search of a Soul*, p. 123). Many scientists, philosophers and educationists agree that a sensate culture without spiritual values leads to the fearful dilemma described by Professor Pitirim A. Sorokin:

> If a person has no strong convictions as to what is right and what is wrong, if he does not believe in any God or absolute moral values, if he no longer respects contractual obligations, and, finally, if his hunger for pleasures and sensory values is paramount, what can guide and control his conduct towards other men? Nothing but his desires and lusts. Under these conditions he loses all rational and moral control, even plain common sense. What can deter him from violating the rights, interests, and well-being of other men? Nothing but physical force. How far will he go in his insatiable quest for sensory happiness? He will go as far as brute force, opposed by that of others, permits. (Pitirim A. Sorokin, *The Crisis of Our Age* [New York, 1944], p. 205)

The austerities of countless saints and sages, disciples and devotees over long centuries demonstrate that sincere spiritual practices generate, sustain, and enhance purity of character and universal harmony.

With maturity, we gain the wisdom that self-control, inner peace, and enlightened living give us deeper, more abiding happiness than outward achievements. Fulfilment comes from within, not from without. Our problems increase if we lack this basic knowledge.

According to Hindu scripture, "Desire is never satisfied by the enjoyment of the objects of desire; it grows more and more as does the fire to which fuel is added" (*Manu*, II, 94).

In his short life and quest for eternal truths, the Dutch philosopher Spinoza (1632-1677) achieved great insights:

> For the things which men, to judge by their actions, deem the highest good are riches, fame or sensual pleasure. Of these the last is followed by satiety and repentance, the other two are never satiated; the more we have, the more we want; while the love of fame compels us to order our lives by the opinions of others. But if a thing is not loved, no quarrels will arise concerning it, no sadness will be felt if it perishes; no envy if another has it, in short no disturbances of the mind. All these spring from the love of that which passes away. But the love of a thing eternal and infinite fills the mind wholly with joy, and is unmingled with sadness. Therefore it is greatly to be desired, and to be sought with all our strength. (Quoted from *The Bhagavadgita*, S. Radhakrishnan, trans. [1997], p. 148)

## DIVINE NATURE OF THE MIND

The pure mind is divine. The pure mind is like milk and the worldly mind is like water. Again, the pure mind is like the sun and the worldly mind is like the cloud. Sri Ramakrishna says, "He alone has become mind, life, and intelligence. We are only His instruments" (*Gospel*, p. 311). Mind is an instrument in God's hand. Pure thoughts sanctify and strengthen the mind. It is not talk, rituals or books that make us virtuous and good but inner strength coming from the sacred power of thought.

The inspired words of God-realized souls destroy our illusion and ignorance and lift our minds to the spiritual heights of supreme insight. The following episode illustrates this truth. Swami Vivekananda was with some of his disciples, one of whom confessed that he was unable to overcome his low-spiritedness. Swamiji told him:

> Then think like this: "Whose child am I? I associate with him and shall I have such weak-mindedness and lowness of spirits?" Stamping down such weakness of mind and heart, stand up, saying, "I am possessed of heroism—I am possessed of a steady intellect—I am a knower of Brahman, a man of illumination." Be fully conscious of your dignity by remembering, "I am the disciple of such and such who is the companion-in-life of Sri Ramakrishna, the conqueror of lust and wealth." This will produce a good effect. He who has not this pride has no awakening of Brahman within him. . . He [Ramprasad] used to say, "Whom do I fear in the world, whose sovereign is the Divine Mother!" Keep such a pride always awake in the mind. Then weakness of mind and heart will no longer be able to approach you. Never allow weakness to overtake your mind. Remember Mahavira, remember the Divine Mother! And you will see that all weakness, all cowardice will vanish at once.
>
> . . . These words were spoken in such an appealing way, that every one stood motionless like a figure painted on canvas and felt as if he were suddenly drawn into the depth of meditation. . . . After some time . . . they regained their normal consciousness. (*C. W.*, VII: 233-34)

Swamiji's power to transform others came from his purity and depth of spiritual experience. The life-giving thoughts of Vedanta enabled him to overcome every obstacle with his Soul-force. Only the power of spiritual thought can overcome pessimistic, depressive, anemic, dull and degraded ideas and replace them with life-sustaining spiritual ones. A ceaseless flow of spiritual thoughts generates the inflowing divine urge, which purifies the mind and strengthens the will for the advent of God and the dawn of spiritual light.

The pure mind aligns nature and matter with spirit. If we want to be successful in our spiritual journey and experience peace and harmony, we must learn to be *in* the world, not *of* the world, by practising detachment. This is the way of attaining maturity. When we have gained knowledge of the nature of pure mind and its function in spiritual life, we will have discovered the science of religion. We must first be convinced that a pure mind is necessary. "The world is a grand moral gymnasium wherein we have all to take exercise so as to become stronger and stronger spiritually," says Swami Vivekananda (*C. W.*, I: 80). The only goal of enlightened, peaceful living is to have a pure mind. A peaceful mind filled with pure thoughts is the only source of real happiness and peace.

## ETERNAL LAWS GOVERN THE MIND

Thought plays a critical and dynamic role in a successful spiritual or secular life. The known or imagined rewards of a profitable worldly life in which we are restless, are perishable. On the other hand, the fruit of spiritual life is imperishable Truth. Swami Vivekananda reconciles the two: "Doing is very good, but that comes from thinking. . . . Fill the brain, therefore, with high thoughts, highest ideals, place them day and night before you, and out of that will come great work" (*C. W.*, II: 86). In modern times, Mahatma Gandhi is one of the noted individuals prominent in our mind. He cultivated his mind in this way and changed the course of history. He broke the mighty British subjugation of India without ever resorting to violence.

Lofty spiritual thoughts teach us to discriminate and impel us to search for the singular "great unknown," which alone fulfils us. Bertrand Russell observed, "The power of thought, in the long run, is greater than any other human power." It is self-evident that whatever we think and do in life shapes our character. Swamiji says, "What we think that our body becomes. Everything is manufactured by thought, and thus we are the manufacturers of our own lives" (*C. W.*, IX: 213).

The confession of a successful American playwright who became a millionaire from the production of his plays, which produced revenues of $200,000 each, may be very instructive. It is from an article by Clive Hirschhorn that was published in a popular San Francisco newspaper after his interview with the renowned playwright, Tennessee Williams:

... He placed his glass (martini) on the table and stared at it unconsciously. There was a pause. He glanced up awkwardly and then peered down at the table again. He looked pale and I asked him if he was not feeling well.

"I never feel well," he said, and smiled a guilty smile of admission. "I might feel better at one particular time or another but I have never, never felt 100 percent. At least, I can't remember when last I did."

I suggested this might be psychological. "Never," he replied emphatically. "I go to an analyst in New York because I have to, and because I need to. There is a big American joke these days about most people going to analysts because it is the thing to do. I go because I have to. My analyst helps me and without him I'd be sunk. I go to him five times a week. That is the only reason why I stay in New York. I hate the place. But I couldn't do it without my analyst. I'd crack up if he weren't around."

Why did he need an analyst so badly, I asked.

"Because I suffer great periods of depression," he said. "ı recently lost a very good friend of mine. This friend had been the scaffold of my life for fifteen years and he died of cancer. He cooked for me, looked after me, and understood me. Without him, I'd never have been able to face up to reality.

"Well, when he died, I went to pieces . . . You see, I'm sentimental, and friendship means a great deal to me. I am middle aged now and friends, really sincere ones, are even harder to come by than before. At one time I had my youth. Now I have nothing.

"I retreated into a shell. For nine months I didn't speak to a living soul. I just clammed up. I would not answer the telephone—which I hate, anyway—and I wouldn't leave the house.

"My analyst has helped me to face life again, and for this I'm naturally very grateful." (Clive Hirschhorn, "Tennessee Williams Speaks of His Fear of Death," *People*, *The California Weekly* section of *The San Francisco Examiner*, Sunday, July 13, 1965)

The death of a friend left a deep impression on Williams' mind. His loss made him very depressed. He became dependent upon his therapist and had to live in a place he did not like because of that dependency. Though successful, famous, wealthy and skilled in his craft, the permanent peace of a stable mind eluded him. He was grateful to his therapist but the science of mental therapy alone did not provide him with a normal, happy and stable life.

Science teaches us physical laws that govern the material world but they have not given us knowledge of the Absolute or true understanding and discrimination. "Every work that we do," Swamiji says, "every movement of the body, every thought that we think, leaves such an impression on the mind-stuff, and even when such impressions are not obvious on the surface, they are sufficiently strong to work beneath the surface, subconsciously. What we are every moment is determined by the sum total of these impressions on the mind" (*C. W.*, I: 54). Raja Yoga, the "Science of sciences," informs us of the laws that rule the mind. Four particularly relevant ones describe the full range of the mind's potential. (1) Mind takes the nature of the thoughts it holds; (2) We see the world subjectively through the prism of our mind; (3) Minds act on each other to afflict or benefit humanity; (4) Mind, transcending thought and senses through the power of imagination and concentration, gains knowledge of the Self.

1. *Mind takes the nature of the thoughts it holds.* The mind is like a sponge. A sponge sucks up any liquid substance it rests on or any that is near it. Similarly, the mind soaks up everything equally, whether it is good or evil, unless it is strengthened by spiritual discrimination. Sri Ramakrishna likened the mind to a white cloth that takes on the colour of the dye applied to it:

> There is such a thing as *abhyasayoga*, yoga through practice. Keep up the practice and you will find that your mind will follow in whatever direction you lead it. The mind is like a white cloth just returned from the laundry. It will be red if you dip it in red dye and blue if you dip it in blue. It will have whatever colour you dip it in. (*Gospel*, p. 539)

More than any other element, thought has the greatest significance in human life, whether it leads to a secular or spiritual end. True spiritual aspirants value the innate power of a pure mind to guide them unerringly towards the spiritual goal of life. Thoughts colour the mind. Mind is the man. Thoughts exert the greatest power over our life. "Mind in its own place and in itself makes a heaven of hell and a hell of heaven" (Milton).

Swami Vivekananda says, "Evil thoughts find the best field in evil people; they are like microbes which germinate and increase only when they find a suitable soil" (*C. W.*, VI: 134). "Evil thoughts, looked at materially, are the disease bacilli. Each thought is a little hammer blow on the lump of iron which our bodies are, manufacturing out of it what we want it to be" (*C. W.*, VII: 20). Mental agonies consume the vitality of the mind and affect the body like a red-hot iron thrust into a jar of cold water. Conversely, pure thoughts find their highest ground in a purified mind and body. The sacred seat of spiritual treasures is an egoless mind filled with pure thoughts.

**2. *We see the world subjectively through the prism of our mind.*** "This very world is seen by the five senses as matter, by the very wicked as hell, by the good as heaven, and by the perfect as God", says Swamiji (*C. W.*, V: 272). Thoughts shape the mind; mind reflects its thoughts on others. Living harmoniously and peacefully in the world improves the quality of the mind. Swami Vivekananda says:

> We are what our thoughts have made us; so take care of what you think. Words are secondary. Thoughts live, they travel far. Each thought we think is tinged with our own character, so that for the pure and holy man, even his jests or abuse will have the twist of his own love and purity and do good. (*C. W.*, VII: 14)

Swamiji warns us to be sentinels of high and noble, not immoral thoughts:

Every vicious thought will rebound, every thought of hatred which you may have thought, in a cave even, is stored up, and will one day come back to you with tremendous power in the form of some misery here. If you project hatred and jealousy, they will rebound on you with compound interest. No power can avert them; when once you have put them in motion, you will have to bear them. Remembering this will prevent you from doing wicked things. (*C. W.*, I: 262)

Christ also warns, "But I say unto you, that whosoever is angry with his brother without a cause shall be in danger of the judgement, and whosoever shall say to his brother, *Raca* ('vain fellow'), shall be in danger of the Council, but whosoever shall say, 'Thou fool,' shall be in danger of hellfire" (Matthew: 5:22).

No amount of organic food will maintain health and purity in an impure mind. Pure thought alone brings health and purity to the mind, with or without the benefit of supplementary aids. In due course, the body and all its actions become pure. "Every good thought that you think or act upon," says Swamiji, "is simply tearing the veil, as it were; and the purity, the Infinity, the God behind, manifests Itself more and more" (*C. W.*, II: 82).

Holy Mother says, "The mind is everything. It is in the mind alone that one feels pure and impure. A man, first of all, makes his own mind guilty and then alone he sees the other man's guilt" (*Thus Spake the Holy Mother*, p. 54).

*3. Minds act on each other to afflict or benefit humanity.* "In this universe where nothing is lost . . ., every thought that is thought, in public or in private, in crowded thoroughfares or in the deep recesses of primeval forests, lives" (*C. W.*, VI: 354).

Most of us are unaware that our thoughts are not at all private or stationary. Thoughts travel far. They are not confined to the thinker or imprisoned in one place—they are universal and non-localized. Thoughts spread out like fine particles with distinct vibrations that move beyond space and time. Swamiji says:

> . . . This mind is a part of the universal mind. Each mind is connected with every other mind. And each mind, wherever it is located, is in actual communication with the whole world . . . Your mind, my mind, all these little minds, are fragments of that universal mind, little waves in the ocean; and on account of this continuity, we can convey our thoughts directly to one another. (*C. W.*, II: 12-13)

Thoughts are always struggling to come alive. Similar minds spontaneously influence each other, behaving with the same affinity as musical instruments. In the phenomenon known as "sympathetic vibration," a keystroke on a perfectly tuned piano stimulates the response of the same identical tone spontaneously heard from a perfectly tuned stringed instrument nearby. Minds attuned to the same spiritual ideal function harmoniously because they receive the power of the same ideal. Swami Vivekananda says:

> Every thought projected from every brain goes on pulsating, as it were, until it meets a fit object that will receive it. Any mind which is open to receive some of these impulses will take them immediately. So, when a man is doing evil actions, he has brought his mind to a certain state of tension and all the waves which correspond to that state of tension, and which may be said to be already in the atmosphere, will struggle to enter into his mind. That is why an evil-doer generally goes on doing more and more

evil. His actions become intensified. Such, also will be the case with the doer of good; he will open himself to all the good waves that are in the atmosphere, and his good actions also will become intensified. We run, therefore, a twofold danger in doing evil: first, we open ourselves to all the evil influences surrounding us; secondly, we create evil which affects others, maybe hundreds of years hence. In doing evil we injure ourselves and others also. In doing good we do good to ourselves and to others as well; and, like all other forces in man, these forces of good and evil also gather strength from outside. (*C. W.*, I: 82)

Infinite thought-power pervades everything. "We are heirs to all the good thoughts of the universe, if we open ourselves to them," Swamiji says (*C. W.*, VII: 20). If we can tune our mind to the highest ideals, we will receive the power of all the positive, elevating thoughts from antiquity to this moment. We inherit the positive thoughts of the ages and pass them on to future generations. Sri Aurobindo says that the mind inhales and exhales thoughts as do lungs the air we breathe. Swamiji says, "Few understand the power of thought. If a man goes into a cave, shuts himself in, and thinks one really great thought and dies, that thought will penetrate the walls of that cave, vibrate through space, and at last permeate the whole human race. Such is the power of thought" (*C. W.*, IV: 177). Thought, therefore, affects existence. Contentedly living within our self-imposed limits, we cannot afford to underestimate the expansive and regenerating capacity of noble thoughts and righteous living. These ideas have great influence even with confirmed agnostics. Colonel Robert G. Ingersoll contributed much to the general welfare of society. He referred to his ethical ideals as "the five gospels" of "Good Living, Cheerfulness, Intelligence, Justice and Liberty."

Wherever great numbers of people have thought and lived nobly according to high ideals, society has been highly blessed. Modern society, however, greatly depends on the "benefits" of technological gadgets. Consumerism encourages material thoughts, which, when they are excessive, eclipse spiritual ideas and thoughts. Swami Vivekananda says, "The more we study the material world the more we tend to become materialized; the more we handle the material world, even the little spirituality which we possessed before vanishes" (*Essentials of Hinduism* [Mayavati, 1947], p. 25).

Cutting edge technology, by itself, offers no proof of a highly advanced society unless the true benefactors of society utilize it. Today's great technological benefits are not matched by great thoughts and ideals. It is used to disseminate ideas inimical to real human progress, rapidly making global society more degenerate and violent.

UNESCO's constitution (1946) has a basic premise: peace must be founded "upon the intellectual and moral solidarity of mankind," and "since wars begin in the minds of men, it is in the minds of men that defenses of peace must be constructed." Maturity gives us insight. Experience shows that spiritual thoughts definitely transform man's savage mentality. The mind soiled by worldliness is transformed through spiritual practices. Holy Mother says:

> One must practise meditation and Japa. That removes the impurities of the mind. One must practise spiritual disciplines such as worship and so forth. As one gets the fragrance of a flower by handling it, as one gets the smell of sandalwood by rubbing it against a stone, in the same way one gets spiritual awakening by constantly thinking of God. But you can realize him now if you become free from desires" (Swami Tapasyananda and Swami Nikhila-

nanda, *Sri Sarada Devi, the Holy Mother* [Mylapore, Madras, 1958], p. 487).

**4. *Mind, transcending thought and senses through the power of imagination and concentration, gains knowledge of the Self.*** Mind's sole purpose is to lead us to the freedom of God-Consciousness or Oneness through knowledge of the Self. Knowledge of the Self means knowledge of Truth, which sets us free. The same power of imagination we harness for worldly ends can be used to remove ignorance. We simply have to change our point of view. A humorous narrative illustrates this principle:

An inebriated gentleman was moving gently along the street carrying in his hand an empty box with perforations in the lid and sides. It appeared that he was carrying some live animal in it. An acquaintance stopped him and asked, "What have you got in the box?" "It is a mongoose," replied the tipsy one. "What on earth for?" "Well, you know how it is with me; I'm not very drunk now, but I shall soon be, and when I am, I see snakes and am scared of them. That is what I have the mongoose for, to protect me." "But good heavens, those are imaginary snakes!" "That is all right," said the drunken man reassuringly, "this is also an imaginary mongoose."

Similarly, all of us need one imagination to counteract another. When we take something imaginary to be real, we need another imagination to counteract the effect of the previous one. The difficulty with us is that we refuse to profit by our experiences and persist in building up fools' paradises, even when they crash one after another and make us suffer no end of troubles. The real reason for all this is our refusal to be de-hypnotized. We prefer to be under the spell of some kind of hypnosis. (Swami Yatiswarananda, *Adventures in Vedanta*, [London, 1961], pp. 140-1)

Swami Vivekananda says, "Imagination properly employed is our greatest friend; it goes beyond reason and is the only light that takes us everywhere" (*C. W.*, VIII: 49). Swamiji says:

> Not one atom can rest until it finds its freedom. . . . Some imaginations help to break the bondage of the rest. The whole universe is imagination, but one set of imaginations will cure another set. Those which tell us that there is sin and sorrow and death in the world are terrible; but the other set which says ever, "I am holy, there is God, there is no pain," these are good and help to break the bondage of the others. The highest imagination that can break all the links of the chain is that of Personal God. (*C. W.*, VII: 99)

Swamiji tells of "something in us which is free and permanent":

> But it is not the body; neither is it the mind. The body is dying every minute. The mind is constantly changing. The body is a combination, and so is the mind, and as such can never reach to a state beyond all change. But beyond this momentary sheathing of gross matter, beyond even the finer covering of the mind is the Atman, the true Self of man, the permanent, the ever free. It is his freedom that is percolating through layers of thought and matter, and in spite of the colourings of name and form, is ever asserting its unshackled existence. It is his deathlessness, his bliss, his peace, his divinity, that shines out and makes itself felt in spite of the thickest layers of ignorance. He is the real man, the fearless one, the deathless one, the free.

Now freedom is only possible when no external power can exert any influence, produce any change. Freedom is only possible to the being who is beyond all conditions, all laws, all bondages of cause and effect. In other words, the unchangeable alone can be free and, therefore, immortal. This Being, this Atman, this real Self of man, the free, the unchangeable, is beyond all conditions, and as such, it has neither birth nor death.

"Without birth or death, eternal, ever-existing is this soul of man." (*C. W.*, IV: 256)

Freedom is not the result of free will, as many believe. Swamiji says, "Free will is a misnomer." (*C. W.*, II: 283) If it is will, it is not free; if it is free, then it is not will. We must understand; indulgence in unrestrained freedom for sensuous gratification or material advantages is not freedom—it is enslavement to lower impulses. Henry Bergson says, "The paradox of freedom is that by the very exercise of freedom we lose it." Swamiji says, "Remember always that only the free have free will; all the rest are in bondage . . . Will as will is bound" (*C. W.*, VII: 99).

These four laws indicate the vast spiritual potential within the mind. Yet, for the vast majority it remains the most neglected, abused and untapped precious resource known to man.

## THE PURPOSE AND FUNCTION OF SYMBOLS IN SPIRITUAL IMAGINATION

However great the abstract idea of God, it does not satisfy the heart of a devotee. Swamiji tells us frankly, "It is easy for men to think that they can understand anything; but when it comes to practical experience, they find that abstract ideas are often very hard to comprehend." Imagination solves this problem by guiding our understanding of the Absolute Reality through concrete names and forms. The entire universe is actually the unfolding of God into various names and forms. All religions have invented symbols as images of the abstract Reality, which "is bound to come clad in visible, tangible, gross garments. This is the law" (*C. W.*, VIII: 149).

All symbols are relative and represent the perfect ideas behind them. Swamiji explains their purpose: "The Hindus have discovered that the Absolute can only be realised, or thought of, or stated, through the relative, and the images, crosses, and crescents are simply so many symbols—so many pegs to hang the spiritual ideas on. . . . it is the attempt of undeveloped minds to grasp high spiritual truths" (*C. W.*, I: 17-18). Spiritual symbols and metaphors invoke the power of our imagination—they are the "stepping stones" to God.

The symbolical method of grasping spiritual ideals has profound meaning. Swamiji says, "Everything in the universe may be looked upon as a symbol. The whole universe is a symbol and God is the essence behind." The idea is to put the symbol that our imagination accepts to its highest use by holding fast to the ideal it represents. Lord Buddha teaches, "Fletchers make the arrow straight, carpenters carve the wood; wise people fashion themselves"—they constantly keep the highest ideal before their minds in every possible way through concentration. Swamiji says:

> Take up one idea. Make that one idea your life — think of it, dream of it, live on that idea. Let the brain, muscles, nerves, every part of your body be full of that idea, and just leave every other idea alone. This is the way to success, and this is the way great spiritual giants are produced" (*C. W.*, I: 177).

The world is ready to give up its secrets if we only know how to knock, how to give it the necessary blow. The strength and force of the blow come through concentration. There is no limit to the power of the human mind. The more concentrated it is, the more power is brought to bear on one point; that is the secret. (*C. W.*, I: 130-1)

## THE PURPOSE OF IMAGINATION IN MEDITATION

For our purposes here, the highest form of concentration is that meditation which brings us nearer to our spiritual dimension or Truth. Imagination is essential in meditation. Swamiji says:

Meditation, you know, comes by a process of imagination. You go through all these processes of purification of the elements—making the one melt into the other, that into the next higher, that into mind, that into spirit, and then you are spirit. . . . So you begin to meditate upon certain external things, objective things, either outside or inside. If you take a long sentence, that is no meditation at all. That is simply trying to get the mind collected by repetition. Meditation means the mind is turned back upon itself. The mind stops all the [thought-waves] and the world stops. Your consciousness expands. Every time you meditate you will keep your growth . . . Work a little harder, more and more, and meditation comes. You do not feel the body or anything else. When you come out of it after the hour, you have had the most beautiful rest you ever had in your life. That is the only way you ever give rest to your system. Not even the deepest sleep will give you such rest as that. The mind goes on jumping even in deepest sleep. Just those few minutes [in meditation] your brain has almost stopped. Just a little vitality is kept up. You forget the body. You may be cut to pieces and not feel it at all. You feel such pleasure in it. You become so light. This perfect rest we will get in meditation. (*C. W.*, IV: 234-5 passim)

The awakened soul rests more truly in meditation than in sleep. Falsity, doubt and fear find no residence in the meditative mind. In pure imagination, we reach the highest state of meditation. In the highest state of meditation we realize the Self or Truth, the goal of Vedanta philosophy. "Philosophy in India," says Swamiji, "means that through which we see God . . . Concrete, generalised, abstract are the three stages in the process of philosophy. The highest abstraction in which all things agree is the One. In religion we have first, symbols and forms; next, mythology; and last, philosophy. The first two are for the time being; philosophy is the underlying basis of all, and the others are only stepping stones in the struggle to reach the Ultimate" (*C. W.*, VII: 49). Swamiji describes the benefits of perfect concentration:

Then comes meditation . . . that is the highest state. . . . When [the mind] is doubtful that is not its great state. Its great state is meditation. It looks upon things and sees things, not identifying itself with anything else. As long as I feel pain, I have identified myself with the body. . . . But the high state will look with the same pleasure or blissfulness upon pleasure or upon pain. . . . Every meditation is direct superconsciousness. In perfect concentration the soul becomes actually free from the bonds of the gross body and knows itself as it is. Whatever one wants, that comes to him. Power and knowledge are already there. The soul identifies itself with that which is powerless matter and thus weeps. It identifies itself with mortal shapes. . . . But if that free soul wants to exercise any power, it will have it. If it does not, it does not come. He who has known God has become God. There is nothing impossible to such a free soul. No more birth and death for him. He is free for ever. (*C. W.*, IV: 226)

One idea alone generates concentration—one-pointed love for knowledge. Our mind easily concentrates on what we love; what we concentrate upon increases our love for it. The popular view claims that we attain peaceful concentration by thinking of what is attractive to the mind, as for example, music, art, natural scenery, etc. According to Pascal, "The sum of evil would be much diminished if men could only learn to sit quietly for five minutes in their room." That counsel is badly needed today. Neglect of concentration on the higher Self undermines our capacity for good. Holy Mother Sarada Devi says, "As one gets the fragrance of a flower by handling it, so does one get spiritual awakening by constantly thinking of God." This is the true meaning and spiritual power of thought, which dispels all unhappiness. Ignorance of our real nature is the cause of our misery.

## "NEVER IS MISERY UNDESERVED"
## IMPROVING THE MIND THROUGH KARMA YOGA

The Law of Karma and the doctrine of will together hold man responsible for his actions. "For whatsoever a man soweth, that shall he also reap" (Galatians, 6:5). World religions unanimously declare the ethical principles of moral idealism and a peaceful attitude that manifest in the pure mind. The mind can make or mar one's life. Swami Vivekananda says:

> We must learn that nothing can happen to us, unless we make ourselves susceptible to it. I have just said, no disease can come to me until the body is ready; it does

not depend alone on the germs, but upon a certain predisposition which is already in the body. We get only that for which we are fitted. Let us give up our pride and understand this, that never is misery undeserved. There never has been a blow undeserved; there never has been an evil for which I did not pave the way with my own hands. We ought to know that. Analyse yourselves and you will find that every blow you have received, came to you because you prepared yourselves for it. You did half, and the external world did the other half: that is how the blow came. That will sober us down. At the same time, from this very analysis will come a note of hope, and the note of hope is: "I have no control of the external world, but that which is in me and nearer unto me, my own world, is in my control. If the two together are required to make a failure, if the two together are necessary to give me a blow, I will not contribute the one which is in my keeping; and how then can the blow come? If I get real control of myself, the blow will never come. (C. W., II: 7-8)

We cannot praise or blame others for what happens to us. Accumulated thoughts and impressions engraved on the mind forge the ancient trail we lengthen with each additional thought, with each new impression. The tendency of the mind—either morally strong and controlled, or morally weak and uncontrolled—creates our destiny. Swami Vivekananda says:

Good and evil have an equal share in moulding character, and in some instances misery is a greater teacher than happiness. In studying the great characters the world has produced, I dare say, in the vast majority of cases, it would be found that it was misery that taught more than

happiness, it was poverty that taught more than wealth, it
was blows that brought out their inner fire more than praise.
(*C. W.*, I: 27)

With maturity, we accept the unavoidable conditions of
life and our inability to change others to please ourselves. We
become aware that our desires gradually change when we
infuse our mind with spiritual thoughts. Only one way purifies
and strengthens the mind—one way alone: strong detachment
from worldliness. This means we must apply our will power
to practise Karma Yoga according to the instructions of the
*Bhagavad Gita* and Swamiji.

The *Bhagavad Gita* (II: 50) teaches us that Yoga is the art
or skill in the performance of an action. The inevitable fruits
of action can be avoided through Karma Yoga. The doctrine
of Karma means that all actions are governed by a law.
Vedanta also proclaims that as we sow, so we reap. "A man
becomes good by good action and bad by bad actions"
(*Brihadaranyaka Upanishad*, III. 2. 13). This is a very logical
and scientific theory. Newton's third law of motion states,
"To every action there is an equal and opposite reaction." This
applies to the spiritual as well as to the physical life. In the
moral world, the law of karma is the counterpart of the law
of cause and effect and the law of conservation of energy in
the physical world. The law of karma rules out fatalism,
accident and chaos in nature. The law of karma is not a law
of retribution; it is not an inexorable law. Divine Grace does
intervene and the effect of karma can be partially or wholly
mitigated. Knowing and accepting this removes bitterness
and cynicism from life. It stands for our freedom of will.
Karma affords us freedom and the opportunity to come out
of the vicious circle of cause and affect. Swami Vivekananda
said, "The only way to come out of bondage is to go beyond

the limitations of law, to go beyond causation" (*C. W.*, I: 98). Karma binds, but unselfish karma liberates us. This is the true significance of Karma Yoga. We are the architects of our fate. Swamiji says:

> ... will is caused by character, and character is manufactured by Karma. As is Karma, so is the manifestation of the will. ... The gigantic will which Buddha and Jesus threw over the world, whence did it come? Whence came this accumulation of power? It must have been there through ages and ages, continually growing bigger and bigger, until it burst on society in a Buddha or a Jesus, even rolling down to the present day.
>
> All this is determined by Karma, work. No one can get anything unless he earns it. This is an eternal law. . . Our Karma determines what we deserve and what we can assimilate. . . But there is such a thing as frittering away our energies. With regard to Karma-Yoga, the *Gita* says that it is doing work with cleverness and as a science; by knowing how to work, one can obtain the greatest results. (C. W., I: 30-31)

In one of his lectures on Karma Yoga, Swamiji said, "We hear 'Be good', and 'Be good,' and 'Be good' taught all over the world. There is hardly a child, born in any country in the world, who has not been told, 'Do not steal,' 'Do not tell a lie,' but nobody tells the child how he can help doing them. Talking will not help him . . . Only when we teach him to control his mind, do we really help him" (*C. W.*, I: 171).

We are conditioned by our past karma. "All that we are is the result of what we have thought," says Swami Vivekananda. The conscious activity of today becomes a future unconscious habit. Delight in newly-found worldly freedom often makes us victims of new habits. The basic teachings of Vedanta can help us before we come to the unhappy realization that our "chains of habit are too weak to be felt till they are too strong to be broken" (Samuel Johnson).

Our actions determine our entire lifestyle, including our habits, thoughts and character. It is the effects of karma that visit us, not any external, irrational agency. Our every action produces two effects. The effect of remorse visits us as the fruit of action long after our action and shapes our destiny. The other effect of action produces a tendency or impression (*samskara*) in our mind, which remembers and continues that action. Swamiji says:

> If good impressions prevail, the character becomes good; if bad, it becomes bad. If a man continuously hears bad words, thinks bad thoughts, does bad actions, his mind will be full of bad impressions; and they will influence his thought and work without his being conscious of the fact. In fact, these bad impressions are always working, and their resultant must be evil, and that man will be a bad man; he cannot help it. The sum total of these impressions in him will create the strong motive power for doing bad actions. He will be like a machine in the hands of his impressions, and they will force him to do evil. Similarly, if a man thinks good thoughts and does good works, the sum total of these impressions will be good; and they, in a similar manner, will force him to do good even in spite of himself. (*C. W.*, I: 54)

This being the fundamental law of our inner nature that shapes our destiny, a moral life of non-attachment and self-restraint is imperative. "The secret of work," to use Swamiji phrase, consists in non-attachment to the work itself and self-restraint. But most people are creatures of habit, and misbegotten habits are very hard to break as we begin to develop our moral character. Those who wish to follow the rugged path of spiritual disciplines which require detachment can only do so by following Swamiji's guidelines:

> The mind, to have non-attachment, must be clear, good, and rational. Why should we practise? Because each action is like the pulsations quivering over the surface of the lake. The vibration dies out, and what is left? The *samskaras*, the impressions. When a large number of these impressions are left on the mind, they coalesce and become a habit. It is said, "Habit is second nature," it is first nature also, and the whole nature of man; everything that we are is the result of habit. That gives us consolation, because, if it is only a habit, we can make and unmake it at any time. The *samskaras* are left by these vibrations passing out of our mind, each one of them leaving its result. Our character is the sum total of these marks, and according as some particular wave prevails one takes that tone. . . Never say any man is hopeless, because he only represents a character, a bundle of habits, which can be checked by new and better ones. Character is repeated habits, and repeated habits alone can reform character. (C. W., I: 207-8)

It is certainly possible to root out evil tendencies from our mind but the fruits of action visit us nonetheless. St. Paul says, "For every man shall bear his own burden" (Galatians 6:5). Swamiji says, ". . . when persons do evil actions, they become more and more evil, and when they begin to do good, they become stronger and stronger and learn to do good at all times" (*C. W.*, I: 81).

## *KNOWLEDGE OF THE SELF THROUGH KARMA YOGA*

Karma Yoga converts our work into a powerful means for our spiritual growth. Swamiji said that every karma—physical, verbal or mental—leaves an indelible mark on one's character. Man is responsible for his own karma. This law rules out fatalism in human life. The attitude of the mind determines the effects of karma on our character.

Work or duty by itself is neither good nor bad. In addition, work or karma by itself is a neutral power. Our inner aptitude, motive and purpose play a great role in shaping our destiny. "The kingdom of God is within you," Christ says (Luke: 17:21). Good work elevates the soul; bad work denigrates its image. Good impulses impel us to creative actions that lead to spiritual development. To break the sinister influence of unhealthy impulses due to our die-hard body-consciousness, we must generate strong will power to counteract the evils of the lower tendencies of the mind. This can be done through work. The important thing is that every one of us can work out his or her own salvation and liberation in this very life through *Karma Yoga* as well as through acquiring sacred knowledge (*Jnana Yoga*), love or worship of God (*Bhakti Yoga*) and union with God (*Raja Yoga*). Each of these paths is a method of gaining knowledge of the Self. Swamiji threw light on this point:

> Now this knowledge, again, is inherent in man. No knowledge comes from outside; it is all inside. What we say a man "knows," should, in strict psychological language, be what he "discovers" or "unveils"; what a man "learns" is really what he "discovers", by taking the cover off his own soul, which is a mine of infinite knowledge. (*C. W.*, I: 28)

In this regard, Swamiji said, "The *Karma Yogi* need not believe in any doctrine whatever. He may not believe even in God, may not ask what his soul is, nor think of any metaphysical speculation. He has got his own special aim of realising selflessness; and he has to work it out himself" (*C. W.*, I: 111).

In Karma Yoga, everything we do can be done as Yoga if we practise self-control, detachment, and offer every action to God—not through fear of punishment or hope of reward but as our worship. Those who follow the precepts of the *Bhagavad Gita* (XVIII: 46) will develop spiritually and live a peaceful life. Swamiji says:

All thought of obtaining return for the work we do hinders our spiritual progress; nay, in the end it brings misery . . . [the] idea of mercy and selfless charity can be put into practice . . . by looking upon work as "worship" in case we believe in a Personal God. Here we give up all the fruits of our work unto the Lord, and worshipping Him thus, we have no right to expect anything from mankind or the work we do. The Lord Himself works incessantly and is ever without attachment. (*C. W.*, I: 59-60)

The central principle of Yoga according to Swamiji is the "manifestation of the Divinity already in man." A true Karma Yogi is expected to demonstrate his awareness of the Divinity underlying all things by serving that Divinity in humanity and offering the fruits of his actions to God. Mahatma Gandhi continues to be the most popular exemplar of Karma Yoga principles in modern times.

The Upanishads give the clarion call to awaken and to keep moving forward courageously to realize our divinity. Many are suffering from spiritual lethargy. Therefore, Swamiji revealed the clear brilliance of the Upanishads in this age of *Kali-Yuga* to awaken us from the spell of physical and moral deterioration:

Arise, Awake! Awake from this hypnotism of weakness. *None* is really weak; the soul is infinite, omnipotent, and omniscient. . . . O ye modern Hindus, de-hypnotise yourselves. . . . Teach yourselves, teach every one his real nature, call upon the sleeping soul and see how it awakes. Power will come, . . . glory will come, and everything that is excellent will come when the sleeping soul is roused to self-conscious activity. (*C. W.*, III: 193)

## REDEEMING LAW OF KARMA AND POWER OF SPIRITUAL THOUGHT

Real wisdom is a weapon against suffering. If we accept our suffering as the fruits of our own karma and calmly submit to God, that attitude is immensely helpful. This sort of calm acceptance of suffering is equivalent to practising religious austerities (*Brihadaranyaka Upanishad*, V. 11. 1). Ordinary persons must struggle to resist the lure of worldliness and to protect themselves as far as possible from increased suffering and pain through prayer and an ethical way of life. "Pain is neither intolerable nor everlasting. . . . It is in the power of the soul to maintain its own serenity" (Marcus Aurelius). True spiritual strength comes only from the Divine; still, we must make every effort to become more spiritual.

We must focus the mind on purity and strength, on infinity and immortality. The strong faculties of imagination, will power and thought are our greatest friend when we seek Truth, and also our greatest enemy when we seek everything that is non-Truth. Swami Vivekananda says:

The same faculty that we employ in dreams and thoughts, namely, imagination, will also be the means by which we arrive at Truth. When the imagination is very powerful, the object becomes visualised. Therefore by it we can bring our bodies to any state of health or disease. When we see a thing, the particles of the brain fall into a certain position like the mosaics of a kaleidoscope. Memory consists in getting back this combination and the same setting of the particles of the brain. The stronger the will the greater will be the success in resetting these particles of the brain. There is only one power to cure the body, and that is in every man. Medicine only rouses this power. Disease is only the manifest struggle of that power to throw off the poison which has entered the body. Although the power to overthrow poison may be roused by medicine, it may be more permanently roused by the force of thought. Imagination must hold to the thought of health and strength in order that in case of illness the memory of the ideal of health may be roused and the particles re-arranged in the position into which they fell when healthy. The tendency of the body is then to follow the brain.

The next step is when this process can be arrived at by another's mind working on us. Instances of this may be seen every day. Words are only a mode of mind acting on mind. Good and evil thoughts are each a potent power, and they fill the universe. As vibration continues so thought remains in the form of thought until translated into action. For example, force is latent in the man's arm until he strikes a blow, when he translates it into activity. We are the heirs of good and evil thought. If we make ourselves pure and the instruments of good thoughts, these will enter us. The good soul will not be receptive to evil thoughts. Evil thoughts find the best field in evil people; they are like microbes which germinate and increase only when they find a suitable soil. (*C. W.*, VI: 133-4)

Will-power guided by selfish, materialistic motives will never give us the mighty virtues of morality and self-control; it cannot enlighten us spiritually or give us peace of mind. Wordsworth's lines are revealing and impel us to cultivate higher spiritual values:

> The World is too much with us; late and soon,
> Getting and spending, we lay waste our powers;
> Little we see in Nature that is ours;
> We have given our hearts away, a sordid boon!

Dynamism, courage, and will-power in and of themselves are not enough to arouse the power of pure thought in the mind. God's grace is also needed. The *Bhagavad Gita* tells us that these come from the Divine alone (*Bhagavad Gita* VII: 8).

Pure thoughts have a propelling force that takes us beyond thought itself to the goal of Soul consciousness. Each soul is potentially divine, but we are not able to harness our potentiality due to our own unspiritual lifestyle. Each of us comes into the world with individual capacities and tendencies. Unless we nurture spiritual thoughts and live a spiritually oriented life, we will not be able to use the divine power that is dwelling within us. Benjamin Franklin wrote in his *Poor Richard's Almanac* (June 1736): "God helps those who help themselves." The parable of the talents in St. Matthew's Gospel teaches us that we go against spiritual law if we waste the talents that God has given us and do not multiply them by using them for good (Matthew 25: 14-29). "For unto every one that hath shall be given, and he shall have abundance; but from him that hath not shall be taken away even that which he hath" (Matthew 25:29).

Sri Ramakrishna's parable of the tethered cow conveys the same message. Farmers tether their grazing cow with a long rope to a strong post in the ground where it can graze. If the cow struggles to reach further, that it might graze beyond the full perimeter of the rope, the farmer may be so pleased that he may extend the length of the rope, tether the cow to another larger grassy area, or even allow the cow to graze freely without a rope. The cow's struggle is rewarded by its master, the farmer. Similarly, our spiritual struggle is rewarded by God. If we do not permit the mind to remain fallow and lose its purity, we shall progress in spiritual life to our greatest benefit.

The great souls who came to the world to relieve human suffering and enlighten humanity, all had to suffer like ordinary mortals. However, living in the constant awareness of God or the Supreme Reality made them impervious to suffering; pain never penetrated their being. We cite Swami Vivekananda, who sustained physical suffering and mental agony throughout his life. One of the greatest spiritual luminaries to appear in the world, Swamiji overcame all suffering and pain through his embodiment of man's true nature as the birthless, deathless Spirit, ever free, perfect and ever pure, which he proclaimed to all. Pain and suffering never really touched him. He lived, taught and worked with fearlessness, faith, reverence and renunciation.

## BENEFITS OF A PURE, CONTROLLED MIND

Purity, therefore, is the mind's greatest attribute. The pure mind is an infinite storehouse of power—all the senses come under its control. Sri Ramakrishna says:

> As long as a man analyses with the mind, he cannot reach the Absolute. As long as you reason with your mind, you have no way of getting rid of the universe and the objects of the senses—form, taste, smell, touch, and sound.

When reasoning stops, you attain the Knowledge of Brahman. Atman cannot be realized through this mind; Atman is realized through Atman alone. Pure mind (*Suddha manas*), Pure intellect (*Suddha buddhi*) and Pure Atman (*Suddha Atman*)—all these are one and the same.

Just think how many things you need to perceive an object. You need eyes; you need light; you need mind. You cannot perceive the object if you leave out any of these three. As long as the mind functions, how can you say that the universe and the "I" do not exist?

When the mind is annihilated, when it stops deliberating pro and con, then one goes into Samadhi, one attains the knowledge of Brahman. (*Gospel*, p. 802)

Only a pure mind is sure to see God. Sri Ramakrishna says:

He is unknowable by the mind engrossed in worldliness. One cannot attain God if one has even a trace of attachment to "woman and gold." But He is knowable by the pure mind and the pure intelligence—the mind and intelligence that have not the slightest trace of attachment. Pure Mind, Pure Intelligence, Pure Atman, are one and the same thing. (*Gospel*, p. 524)

Spiritual life minimizes stress through effective control of the mind. Spiritual thoughts strengthen the mind; worldly thoughts weaken it. The best way to strengthen the mind and lead a moral life of virtue is to keep the mind on God as His devotee. Swamiji says, "Excess of knowledge and power, without holiness, makes human beings devils" (*C. W.*, I: 425). Nobel Prize-winning poet and essayist Maurice Maeterlinck (1862-1949) points this out in the Preface to one of his books:

"The greatest engineer, mathematician, physician or space scientist can be an exploiter or a senseless fool. People sometimes don't observe this or they forget it" (Maurice Maeterlinck, *The Great Beyond*, [New York, 1947]).

Ignorance enslaves us; control of the mind leads to freedom from bondage. Swamiji says, "When your mind has become controlled, you have control over the whole body; instead of being a slave to this machine, the machine is your slave. Instead of this machine being able to drag the soul down, it becomes its greatest helpmate" (*C. W.*, I: 265). "When the mind is free from activity or functioning, it vanishes and the Self is revealed. This state has been described by the commentator Shankara as . . . [the] supersensuous perception" (*C. W.*, VI: 475).

## *"IF MATTER IS POWERFUL, THOUGHT IS OMNIPOTENT"*

The world is the product of thought. Thought precedes action; good (and therefore liberating actions) or evil (and therefore binding actions) are the external expression of inner thoughts. Spiritual thoughts strengthen the mind bound by worldliness. Sri Ramakrishna says:

> Bondage is of the mind, and freedom is also of the mind. A man is free if he constantly thinks: "I am a free soul. How can I be bound, whether I live in the world or in the forest? I am a child of God, the King of Kings. Who can bind me?" If bitten by a snake, a man may get rid of its venom by saying emphatically, "There is no poison in me." In the same way, by repeating with grit and determination, "I am not bound, I am free," one really becomes so—one really becomes free. (*Gospel*, p. 138)

Swamiji emphatically says:

Do you know how much energy, how many powers, how many forces are still lurking behind that frame of yours? What scientist has known all that is in man? Millions of years have passed since man first came here, and yet but one infinitesimal part of his powers has been manifested. Therefore, you must not say that you are weak. How do you know what possibilities lie behind that degradation on the surface? You know but little of that which is within you. For behind you is the ocean of infinite power and blessedness. . . .

Fill yourselves with the ideal; whatever you do, think well on it. All your actions will be magnified, transformed, deified, by the very power of the thought. If matter is powerful, thought is omnipotent. Bring this thought to bear upon your life, fill yourselves with the thought of your almightiness, your majesty, and your glory. (C. W., II: 301-2 passim)

Allowing these life-giving, noble ideals and thoughts to regulate and direct the mind prevents us from succumbing to bad impulses. Almost every Indian school of philosophy accepts the concept of *pratipaksabhavana*, the removal of evil thoughts through meditation on opposite, pure ones. In many Indian systems of thought, elimination of evil thoughts has always been the springboard for the self to attain liberation.

According to Swamiji, action is external motion and human thought is internal motion (*C. W.*, VII: 421). Perception begins with the mind, which is subtle matter. ". . . Mind is much finer matter than the external instruments . . . The mind is an instrument, as it were, in the hands of the soul, through which the soul catches external objects" (*C. W.*, I: 135).

## FOUR NOTABLE EXAMPLES OF
## INNER TRANSFORMATION

Capacities differ; not everyone is interested in the lives of the saints, from whose example we learn of inner transformation. If we take a little trouble to think about how we can improve our life, we will realize that millions of others have already done this through an inner spiritual struggle to improve their character. They demonstrate the triumph of human spirit over adversity. The world is full of outstanding examples of self-made men and women with deep faith in the indwelling Soul. Of great worth, they are valuable to humanity. A glimpse of a few notable men and women who rose above the common ranks uplifts our drooping spirit.

### *LEO TOLSTOY (1828-1910)*

Some rare, extraordinary souls become bored and depressed when they realize that they lack an intellectually convincing, morally uplifting and spiritually fulfilling scheme of life. Tolstoy was one of them. At fifty, he was at the peak of worldly success and had not encountered any grave difficulty. Still, he began to feel an inner emptiness for not having found out the meaning of life. He carried this heavy cross within himself for two years and ultimately began scheming to end his life. He pondered the means of the bullet or the rope. William James quoted Tolstoy's reminiscences of that period:

> I remember one day in early spring, I was alone in the forest, lending my ear to its mysterious noises. I listened, and my thought went back to what for these three years it was always busy with—the quest of God. "But the idea of him," I said, "how did I ever come by the idea?"

And again there arose in me, with this thought, glad aspirations towards life. Everything in me awoke and received a meaning . . . "Why do I look farther?" a voice within me asked. "He is there: he, without whom one cannot live. To acknowledge God and to live are one and the same thing. God is what life is. Well, then! Live, seek God, and there will be no life without him . . ."

After this, things cleared up within me and about me better than ever, and the light has never wholly died away. I was saved from suicide. Just how and when the change took place I cannot tell. But as insensibly and gradually as the force of life had been annulled within me, and I had reached my moral deathbed, just as gradually and imperceptibly did the energy of life come back. And what was strange was that this energy that came back was nothing new. It was my ancient juvenile force of faith, the belief that the sole purpose of my life was to be *better*. I gave up the life of the conventional world, recognizing it to be no life, but a parody on life, which its superfluities simply keep us from comprehending. (Quoted from William James, *The Varieties of Religious Experience* [London and Bombay, 1902], p. 185)

Tolstoy's inner transformation did not happen overnight because of a powerful spiritual experience; it came because for many years, he remained a man of enduring faith in higher ideals. He searched relentlessly throughout his adult life for a universal concept of religion that he could embrace. Towards the end of his life, he came into contact with the teachings of Sri Ramakrishna and Swami Vivekananda. By 1909, he had already culled one hundred sayings of Sri Ramakrishna. By the time of his death, Russia's mystic literary voice had become her herald of India's spiritual thoughts.

## DEVENDRANATH TAGORE (1817-1905)

Almost in the same period, Devendranath Tagore, father of the great poet Rabindranath Tagore, was feeling deeply depressed and markedly indifferent to the world. He was disenchanted with it. A mysterious longing for a greater reality took hold of him. One day he noticed a stray piece of paper fluttering past him. He captured it and saw some Sanskrit verses on it. It was a page from the *Isa Upanishad*. He referred it to a Sanskrit scholar who translated the first verse for him: "Our whole universe is permeated by the Spirit. Receive Him by renouncing all desire for worldly pleasure. Take delight in Him alone" (*Isa Upanishad*, I. 1). This caused such a tremendous upturn in his mind that his depression immediately vanished; he felt transformed. He wrote:

> When I learned the explanation, nectar from paradise streamed upon me. I had been eager to receive sympathetic response from men; now a divine voice had descended from heaven to respond to my heart of hearts, and my longing was satisfied. Could men give any such response? The very mercy of God Himself descended into my heart. My faith in God took deep root; in lieu of worldly pleasure I tasted henceforth divine joy. (*Autobiography of Maharshi Devendranath Tagore*. English translation. Quoted from *Adventures in Vedanta*, p. 89)

## WILLIAM JAMES (1842-1910)

The distinguished American psychologist and philosopher, William James, was Tolstoy's contemporary. He was ill most of his life, which made him so depressed that he contemplated suicide more than once in his life. He felt that no one is fully human who has *not* contemplated it. He had a spiritual experience in his later years that gave him a "triumphant sense of certainty." This led him to a bold, new philosophy: to "hold ourselves erect and keep our hearts unshaken" in the dangerous game of life. He decided that by exercising his free will he could choose to save himself in spite of his suffering: "My life shall [be built upon] doing and suffering and creating . . . I must *do* my man-business, bravely" (Henry and Dana Lee Thomas, *Living Adventures in Philosophy* [New York, 1954], p. 271). By developing his character, he re-entered the stream of life with courage.

Perhaps his heroic character-formation was influenced by his friendship with Swami Vivekananda during Swamiji's informal talks on Comparative Religion at the Cambridge Conferences in the 1890s. In his *Varieties of Religious Experience*, James quoted Swamiji's dynamic words regarding man's inner divinity. James' favourite quotation became, "Son of man, stand upon thy feet, and I will speak unto thee" from the prophet Ezekiel. These words supported his idea of a bold, free will and his conviction that salvation lay within oneself. His pragmatic philosophy stresses cooperation and a contented mind. It rejects competitiveness, material success and fame as the exclusive goals of life. The "cash value" of his philosophy, he claimed, was a healthy mind and body, courage, and harmonious relationships with others, especially one's family. His philosophy matured in later years and he gained "a stronger incentive for living, a wiser tolerance towards others, a clearer outlook upon the universe, wider horizons, deeper satisfactions and greater peace" (Quoted from *Living Adventures in Philosophy*, pp. 272-3). In *The Varieties of Religious Experience*, James wrote:

. . . our normal waking consciousness . . . is but one special
type of consciousness, whilst all about it, parted from it

by the filmiest of screens; there lie potential forms of consciousness entirely different. We may go through life without suspecting their existence; but apply the requisite stimulus, and at a touch they are there in all their completeness . . . No account of the universe in its totality can be final which leaves these other forms of consciousness quite disregarded.

He once said, "The greatest discovery of my generation is that human beings can alter their lives by altering their attitude of mind."

## VIKTOR FRANKL (1905-1997)

Dr. Viktor Frankl was a professor of psychiatry and neurology at the University of Vienna. He spent three bleak years at Auschwitz and other Nazi prisons, forcibly stripped of all sense of humanity and every possession. He gained his freedom only to discover that everyone in his family had been exterminated in the prison camps except his sister. During these terrible ordeals, he deliberately chose a life-saving attitude: he would sublimate his degradation and suffering by thinking of the higher meaning of life. He averted all thoughts of suicide and lived through the harshest conditions. He and a few other physically weak prisoners like himself managed to survive the Nazi camps because of their conviction that they were souls tethered to their bodies. Others who were physically stronger and healthier but who lacked this strong conviction of the soul consciousness, fatally succumbed to stress and suffering.

Frankl put forward the value that man is responsible for his life—"life itself asks questions of man . . . he has to respond by being responsible; and he can answer to life by answering *for* his life"—that is, by discovering the meaning of his life (Viktor E. Frankl, *The Doctor and the Soul* [England, 1973], p.73). The whole task of existential analysis, according to Frankl, is through the "right activity" of reorienting oneself to the unique meaning of life (Ibid., p. 237). Under "the hammer blows of fate, in the white heat of suffering" this value relieves us of "ignoble misfortune" (blameworthy destiny); it raises our consciousness and allows us to perceive danger from the higher perspective of inevitable, immutable destiny or "noble misfortune" (Ibid., pp. 114-115).

Prisoners without this "will to meaning" perished in the camps. Frankl recognized that what these camp prisoners suffered is what we all suffer, when we come face to face with death and suddenly realize that we have "nothing to lose except [our] so ridiculously naked life." Powerful heightened emotions and frozen indifference alternately beset us. Gordon W. Allport describes this in his preface to Frankl's book, *Man's Search for Meaning*:

> . . . First to the rescue comes a cold detached curiosity concerning one's fate. Swiftly, too, come strategies to preserve the remnants of one's life, though the chances of surviving are slight. Hunger, humiliation, fear and deep anger at injustice are rendered tolerable by closely guarded images of beloved persons, by religion, by a grim sense of humor, and even by glimpses of the healing beauties of nature—a tree or a sunset. . . . to live is to suffer, to survive is to find meaning in the suffering. (*Man's Search for Meaning*, pp. x-xi)

Loving images, humour and healing glimpses are not sufficient to establish in us the strong will to defy death and the wish to live. Something more is needed: the ability to find and cling to the larger meaning of suffering and injustice,

5

which play an inevitable role in life. We do not want to suffer merely; we want to survive suffering by finding its meaning and purpose. Each of us must discover this for ourselves. The most painful experience can reveal to us the same purpose of life experienced by others, that a higher spiritual power dwells within us. Due to this spiritual power within us, we are able to elevate our thoughts and realize that we are immortal, infinite, and eternal. This enables us to rise above all suffering. Knowledge of our divinity brings meaning and purpose to the suffering that we cannot change or avoid in life.

The Greek word "Logos," means "spirit" and "meaning." Frankl chose the word "logotherapy" when he founded his new science of existential analysis. Logotherapy distinguishes between the spirit and instincts. It focuses on the "meaning of human existence as well as on man's search for such a meaning" and treats our frustrated hopes for a meaningful existence in spiritual terms. Unlike other western therapies, it deals with our instinctive, unconscious side in the same spiritual terms.

Logotherapy took shape in Frankl's mind during his struggle to survive in various Nazi camps. One of its basic concepts is the essential, spiritual aspect of human existence gathered from the fruits of his experience. It is concerned with the whole concept of man and our search for a higher meaning in every circumstance of life. Logotherapy initially confronts patients with their lack of awareness of the higher meaning of life. It then helps them to become aware of the existential dilemma that is behind their distress and to rise to the great challenge of finding and pursuing the higher meaning of life.

Viktor Frankl became the president of the Austrian Medical Society of Psychotherapy, Professor of Psychiatry and Neurology at the University of Vienna. In due course, he went to live in America. He taught psychiatry and neurology at the U. S. International University in San Diego, California, and was a visiting professor at the Harvard University Summer School as well as visiting Clinical Professor of Psychiatry at Stanford University Medical School (Viktor E. Frankl, *The Doctor and the Soul*, front pages, i). The deep inspiration he received while in the Nazi camps and the profound light it shed on the meaning of life was the subject of many of his lectures, which drew very large audiences. He was invited to lecture at the Royal Society of Medicine in London, made at least thirty-two lecture tours in the United States as well as three lecture tours around the world. He also spoke to large audiences in Argentina, Australia, Ceylon, India, Israel, Japan, Hawaii, Mexico, South Africa, Puerto Rico, China and Costa Rica (Ibid.)

A feverishly hectic, reckless and restless individual is always emotionally impaired. Our busy lives lack the dimension of depth. Frankl wrote, "It is self-evident that belief in a super-meaning—whether as a metaphysical concept or in the religious sense of Providence—is of the foremost psychotherapeutic and psychohygienic importance" (*The Doctor and the Soul*, p. 49). The testimony of many great souls is that the faith that springs from inner strength sustains us through otherwise intolerable suffering. Strong faith in God is helpful. His personal experience and clinical observations convinced Frankl that man's search for a higher meaning is a primary force: "The will to meaning is in most people *fact*, not faith."

Frankl contrasted his *will to meaning*—which is supported by higher spiritual values, with Freud's *will to pleasure* and Adler's *will to power.* He recognized that we have an inner capacity greater than instinctual, defensive reactions with which to face suffering: "Man . . . is able to live and even to die for the sake of his ideals and values!" (*Man's Search for*

*Meaning*, p. 155). He loved to quote Nietzsche, who wrote, "He who has a *why* to live can bear with almost any *how*." Goethe says, "There is no predicament that we cannot ennoble either by doing or enduring." This gives us a correct perspective on suffering, some of which are avoidable or unavoidable. Both are a part of our individual and common destiny with others. We can do something about what is avoidable but can only choose to endure or succumb to unavoidable events.

## MAN'S ADVERSITY IS GOD'S OPPORTUNITY
## FOUR WHO UNDERSTOOD THE DEEPER
## MEANING OF SUFFERING

Divine Power being behind the mind, there are some people who, in spite of mental stress or physical abnormality, have enough mental resources to ignore them. Having acknowledged and submitted to their inner spiritual dimension, they call upon it with the confidence of faith. Having tapped the infinite resource of that Power lying within them, they are able to calmly face and endure the shocks and provocations of life without brooding and wallowing in self-pity, without succumbing to anger, fear, or depression. They have understood the deeper meaning of suffering, which is a means to correct our view of life, an opportunity to discover and awaken the spiritual dimension lying dormant within. Famed personality, Helen Keller, perhaps put it best: "I thank God for my handicaps, for, through them, I have found myself, my work, and my God" (*The Best Years of My Life*, p. 92).

Such personalities encourage and bring hope to many others. The transformed lives of four individuals offer relevant testimony in this regard. Louise L. Hay is a Wellness Specialist and New Age metaphysical lecturer. She is a best-selling author of twenty books on self-healing, including *Heal Your Body*, which have been translated into twenty-nine different languages in thirty-five countries. She built her optimistic philosophy of life by releasing all sense of blame, cultivating forgiveness, nurturing a sense of universal gratitude, and relying on the "tremendous Power and Essence of life that many call God." Louise Hay had suffered poverty, neglect, and emotional and physical abuse from a tender age and was raped at the age of five. She reacted to all this by living an immoral life. A baby girl that was born to her out of wedlock when she was sixteen had to be given away to a childless couple because she could not provide it with a loving, stable home life. Thus, she was also deprived of the joys of motherhood. She travelled to New York, where she became a high-fashion model. She met and married her husband, who left her after fourteen years of marriage for another woman. Finally, after her divorce and just when she felt she had experienced all the suffering that she could bear, she was diagnosed with vaginal cancer, a direct result of her profligate lifestyle of so many years. She now became convinced that if she could change her way of thinking, she could change her life for the better. She ultimately realized that she "must go within to find a cure." She painstakingly began drumming the words "I'll be better; all is well" with a positive attitude into her consciousness. She supported this idea by also taking better care of herself physically, through an improved diet and detoxification after consulting with a nutritionist. She began taking responsibility for her own healing and summoned her inner power of positive thoughts to "clear away the mental pattern that created this cancer." She cured herself without surgery or the treatment of doctors and overcame the obstacles in her life by developing love and compassion for herself and others. She took care of her helpless elderly mother, and rescued and helped her abused sister. With great ingenuity, she recovered and began to earn money as a counsellor in New York. Today, her foundation, Hay House, Inc., disseminates various forms of media on the subject of healing. Her special meditations of positive affirmation and numerous books have helped many others. In *You Can Heal Your Life* (First Indian Paperback ed., 2000) the author's dedication reads, "May this offering help you find the place within where you know your own self-worth, the part of you that is pure love and self-acceptance." She is still publishing in her eighties. One of her most recent books is *The Times of Our Lives: Extraordinary True Stories of Synchronicity, Destiny, Meaning and Purpose* (2007). She has helped thousands of individuals to discover and use their full creative potential for healing and self-growth. She is a much sought after counsellor, lecturer and healer living in southern California.

Many other well-known personalities demonstrated this strength in their lives. However, there are also millions of common people, less known or nameless to posterity. Ennobled by their spontaneous joyous feeling, accommodating attitude, and sense of humour and cheerfulness, they provide encouragement and hope to others. For example, a crippled veteran of World War I was able to make a significant contribution to others. Newton Baker, former Secretary of War under President Wilson, discovered this veteran during a routine visit to a Federal hospital where the most seriously wounded American soldiers were treated. He was a young soldier, whose wounds might have permanently dispirited him. His face was mutilated beyond recognition. He had lost both his eyes and legs, and one arm. Remarkably, he shone with a spiritual radiance. His courage and inner strength had helped him to accept the unavoidable suffering and to rise above it. The hospital staff took him around in a wheelchair to visit other patients, who were encouraged and consoled by his cheerfulness and radiant spirit. He was never a problem or burden to anyone. He married the woman who had been his nurse. A few years later, the veteran's enlightened attitude and undefeated spirit earned him academic excellence at the prestigious Johns Hopkins University. It so happened, that Mr. Baker was one of its trustees. In this capacity, he received a letter from the president, who "wished to do an unusual thing, to hold a mid-semester convocation to bestow the degree of Doctor of Philosophy upon a young man who, though heavily handicapped, had done one of the most brilliant pieces of work at the University. His name was that of the crippled veteran." Mr. Baker was greatly surprised and pleased that the honoree was none other than the spirited, determined crippled veteran he had met years before. It was clear that he had not become a problem to the world. His great moral achievement was that he had become "part of the answer" (*Light from Many Lamps*, Lillian Eichler Watson, ed. [New York, 1951], p. 94).

Another example was Harold Russell, a young sergeant paratrooper in World War II, who lost both hands in an accident at his training camp. At first, feeling helpless, bitter and terrified, he fell into a deep depression. It so happened that an elderly World War I veteran, Major Charley McGonegal, had overcome similar injuries with the help of an inspiring quote from Ralph Waldo Emerson. The Major visited the sergeant in the hospital and told him that the greatest obstacle he had to overcome was *himself*. He shared the Emerson quote with the young patient: "For everything you have missed, you have gained something else." This was helpful, but still the sergeant wavered. Then the Major eased the young patient's despair with these hopeful words: "You are not crippled; you are merely handicapped." Together, these two wonderful statements became a powerful force in the young man's mind. He completely changed his attitude. His "priceless wealth of the spirit" transformed his weakness and sense of inferiority into his greatest strength. He stopped resisting his handicap and accepted it. Eventually, he became a movie star, won two Academy Awards, and authored books that appeared on the Best-seller list. He learned to drive and play the piano. Moreover, he enjoyed the benefits of a "fully rich and rewarding" life "of meaning and depth" that included marriage and a family. He had learned, "It is not what you have lost but what you have left that counts." His shining example encouraged thousands of handicapped men and women. Millions who saw him on the screen and read his books and humble autobiography have been inspired to lead better lives by his cheerful, courageous and noble example.

These two brave men conquered their fears through their courage. In spite of suffering terrible handicaps and disfigurement, they used their powers of inspired thought and will to make themselves radiant, cheerful, and mentally strong in order to live meaningful lives and become an inspiring example to many other healthy as well as handicapped people (*Light from Many Lamps*, pp. 88-94 passim). They learned, rightly, to endure their hardships and make progress in life.

All these examples illustrate the efficacy and power of the mind guided by spiritual ideals to heal the body and to transform and elevate a person to a more purposeful, meaningful life. Medical treatment and health interventions are helpful strategies in curing illness, but they are body-dependent, not spirit-dependent. They surely have their place in the overall treatment of disease but they do not provide the inner wisdom and spiritual strength that enables us to deal with stress and suffering in our lives. Drugs can alleviate pain and the threat of death from complications of surgery but patients learn little about how to cope with these problems in a lasting and secure way. Without the added spiritual benefit of elevating ideas and thoughts that give us a deep understanding of the role of suffering in life, traditional medicine, by itself, is an inferior strategy for healthy living.

This is beautifully illustrated by Dr. Larry Dossey's astonishing account of our fourth example, a patient whom he calls "Nancy." She presented herself to him when she was twenty-nine years old and suffering from recurrent chest pain. For the last five years, she had been incapacitated by costochondritis, with swelling, redness and extreme pain in the sternocostochondral areas of her chest (areas where cartilage joins the ribs to the breastbone). Though many patients find relief with the help of pain-killing medicine, rest and applied heat, Nancy did not. Several times a year, she would find herself unable to function, because any movement of her limbs would cause excruciating pain. Dr. Dossey's diagnostic tests in the hospital returned normal results for Nancy, baffling him. The severe episode of costochondritis he was treating gradually lessened but she suffered four more relapses that year, her first in his care. Rheumatitis and thoracic cancer were suspected in her case but not confirmed by further tests. Nancy rejected the traditional biopsies and surgery to the affected areas of her chest that were recommended by the surgeon. Several pain control methods she tried proved as ineffective as everything else she had tried. Two years later, Dr. Dossey still could not help his patient. In one of her routine visits, she reported something very unusual to him. In the earliest stages of one of her typical episodes when a nagging pain in the chest at the edge of the sternum always appeared, a thought entered her mind with peculiar force: "The problem still exists. Medical science can do nothing for me. I have to handle this myself." She immediately placed herself in a relaxed position and began focusing on her pain.

After some time, it lessened and disappeared. She had discovered that combining deep relaxation and intense concentration on the area of her pain brought her total relief from her symptoms. Where traditional therapies had failed, Nancy's willingness to use her own mental power of suggestion cured her. She applied the effective method she had discovered from within and slowly reordered and restored her entire organism with this psychophysical approach. Thereafter, whenever the symptoms would appear, she diverted her mind to the higher wisdom of her intuition and counteracted the obstacles to her well-being (Larry Dossey, M. D., *Space, Time and Medicine* [Boulder & London, 1982], pp. 93-5).

When we grasp the moral and spiritual significance of suffering, we give it a place of honour. Viktor Frankl says:

> The destiny a person suffers . . . This "right" enduring is the kind which constitutes a moral achievement; only such unavoidable suffering is meaningful suffering. This moral achievement implicit in suffering is something that the ordinary person in his simple, straightforward way knows quite well" (*The Doctor and the Soul*, p. 115).

## ESCAPE FROM THE PRISON OF THE EGO

We are not meant to live superficially and egotistically, like "a feverish selfish clod of ailments and grievances" (George Bernard Shaw). "An overpowerful ego is a prison from which a man must escape if he is to enjoy the world to the full. A capacity for genuine affection is one of the marks of the man who has escaped from this prison of the self" (Bertrand Russell, *The Conquest of Happiness* [New York, 1971], p. 185). Spiritual life essentially dwarfs egocentric life. When we expand ourselves spiritually, we break away from self-absorption.

There is no magic formula for self-expansion. "It is an outcome of poise and self-reliance," writes Bertrand Russell, and "demands what may be called mental integration . . . that the various layers of a man's nature, conscious, subconscious, and unconscious, work together harmoniously and are not engaged in perpetual battle" (*The Conquest of Happiness*, p. 106). Most of us know the satisfaction that harmony gives to others as well as to ourselves.

Emotional poise helps us to live more peacefully and purposefully. Dr. James Gordon Wilkey came to this conclusion when he compared his own lack of stress despite his busy priestly work schedule to his parishioners' high levels of stress. Many of them felt helplessly "overdriven, overburdened and overtired" by their attachment to the responsibilities of work and family, dictated by modern living. Strain, nervousness and anxiety had made them extremely upset, mentally and emotionally. As he pondered on the theme, "Gaining Emotional Poise," that he chose for that Sunday's sermon, an hourglass appeared to his imagination:

What is the true picture of your life? Imagine that there is an hourglass on your desk. Connecting the bowl at the top with the bowl on the bottom is a tube so thin that only one grain of sand can pass through it at a time.

That is the true picture of your life, even on a super-busy day. The crowded hours come to you always one moment at a time. That is the only way they *can* come. The day may bring many tasks, many problems, strains, but invariably, they come in single file.

You want to gain emotional poise? Remember the hourglass, the grains of sand dropping one by one . . . (*Light from Many Lamps*, pp. 219-21)

His entire well-received sermon was published in *Best Sermons, 1944 Selection* and quoted from in the popular *Reader's Digest* (Ibid).

Communion with and devotion to our spiritual ideal is essential religious experience. The little ego is inflated by what belongs to it; the enlightened self is made significant by what it belongs to. Respecting the higher Self, we live righteously and control our emotions. The noble aptitude of searching for a meaningful life is itself a great privilege. Love for the inner Self makes us heroic. "Every sort of energy and endurance, of courage and capacity for handling life's evils is set free in those who have religious faith" (William James).

Spiritual grace is not limited to saints or renowned personalities; it is universal. The simple, traditional religious values of ordinary people help keep religion alive: "These sincere believers are valuable to the world because they keep alive the conviction that God is more important than matter" (Bertrand Russell).

## SUPREME VALUE OF PRAYER AND FAITH

"Prayer is an act of devotion influencing the very depth of the soul, permeating the whole life and shaping every action," writes a Christian mystic. Dr. Alexis Carrel (1873-1944), a physician at Rockefeller Institute, won the Nobel Prize in Medicine in 1911. The original British edition of his book, *Man, the Unknown*, sold over 100,000 copies and was translated into twelve languages. Dr. Carrel spoke about the value of prayer: "Prayer is the most powerful form of energy one could generate. Prayer, like radium, is a source of luminous, self-generating energy. When we pray, we link ourselves with the inexhaustible motive power that spins the Universe, our human deficiencies are filled and we arise strengthened and repaired." Prayer should be reinforced by meditation.

All of us experience a measure of sickness, depression and personal loss. Some of us fare better through these ordeals than others, because we have learned to turn our attention away from ourselves. We prefer, not to brood in self-pity, but to accept the inevitable as a unique opportunity to express our utter dependence on God through prayer. Dr. Carrel says:

Prayer should be understood, not as a mere mechanical recitation of formulas, but as a mystical elevation, an absorption of consciousness in the contemplation of a principle both permeating and transcending our world. Such a psychological state is not intellectual. It is incomprehensible to philosophers and scientists, and inaccessible to them. But the simple seem to feel God as easily as the heat of the sun or the kindness of a friend. The prayer which is followed by organic effects is of a special nature. First, it is entirely disinterested. Man offers himself to God. He stands before Him like the canvas before the painter or the marble before the sculptor. At the same time, he asks for His grace, exposes his needs and those of his brothers in suffering . . . The modest, the ignorant, and the poor are more capable of this self-denial than the rich and the intellectual. When it possesses such characteristics, prayer may set in motion a strange phenomenon, the miracle. (*Man, the Unknown*, pp. 141-2)

## PHENOMENAL CURES THROUGH THE HOLY MIRACLE AND REPENTANCE

Phenomenal cures that occur in holy places like Lourdes, France, demonstrate the influence of the spiritually oriented mind on the body. The medical and scientific communities have not understood the significance of this influence, despite carefully documented scientific evidence. Two stone buildings at Lourdes serving as rudimentary hospitals admit from 1,000 to 1,500 patients every three or five days. Patients willingly endure crowded, damp conditions and minimal care that increases their suffering. Their hope and faith in a higher Being far outweighs the loss of hospital services and pain relief given to them at home. There is greater patient confidence and contentment within the walls of the hospitals at Lourdes than within the walls of more modern, well-equipped ones.

Once or twice a day, patients are taken to the Grotto, where there is a figure of the Lady of Lourdes, signifying the compassionate healing aspect of Mary, the mother of Jesus. After bathing in the Grotto's miraculous waters, they are carried to the semicircular ramps of the church. There they may lie in the sun or rain for hours on end, while hundreds of thousands of pilgrims (arriving in groups for the prescribed three to five days) proceed around them, praying with deep devotion. The Blessed Sacrament is passed over the patients. This is the background for the miraculous cure or relief experienced by some patients.

Annually, fewer than two hundred of the million or more pilgrims are cured, according to documentation dating back to 1888. The Medical Bureau established at Lourdes confirms and documents purely organic cures. Many cured patients do not need further confirmation of what they have just experienced; they do not bother to report their cure to the Bureau. All of them leave Lourdes filled with an inner quietude and humility that often lasts a lifetime.

This is Dr. Carrel's informed view of the significant phenomenon:

> Miraculous cures seldom occur. Despite their small number, they prove the existence of organic and mental processes that we do not know. They show that certain

mystic states, such as that of prayer, have definite effects. They are stubborn, irreducible facts, which must be taken into account. . . .

The most important cases of miraculous healing have been recorded by the Medical Bureau of Lourdes . . . patients have been cured almost instantaneously of various afflictions, such as peritoneal tuberculosis, cold abscesses, osteitis, suppurating wounds, lupus, cancer, etc. . . . In a few seconds, a few minutes, at the most a few hours, wounds are cicatrized, pathological symptoms disappear, appetite returns . . . The miracle is chiefly characterized by an extreme acceleration of the processes of organic repair . . . the rate . . . is much greater than the normal one. The only condition indispensable to the occurrence of the phenomenon is prayer. But there is no need for the patient himself to pray, or even to have any religious faith. It is sufficient that someone around him be in a state of prayer. Such facts are of profound significance. (*Man, The Unknown*, pp. 142-3)

The soul cured of its troubled conscience through repentance is no less a phenomenal cure than the miracles of Lourdes. A guilty conscience plagues millions of people. Some immoral action they committed weighs mightily on their mind and heart. They suffer keenly in this lonely state. Unable to confess their horrible deed to others, they need God's mercy, knowingly or unknowingly. Their psychic malady is that "Unnatural deeds do breed unnatural troubles; infected minds to their deaf pillows will discharge their secrets" (*Macbeth*). They desperately want to end their unbearable remorse for which there is no external recourse. They feel the urgent need to confess, to make amends, and to bring peace to their mind. In one shared aspect with the physically impaired patients at

Lourdes, they feel that no privation is too great to bear, if only they can be relieved of their mental woe.

In *The Way of a Pilgrim*, the humble unnamed wanderer who prayed without ceasing came across an emaciated, dying old man, formerly Prince X——. He expressed a dire need to reveal his crime against his former valet, who died from his master's angry blow to the head. At first indifferent to his crime, eventually, he was haunted night and day by the frightening apparition of the valet appearing in his dreams and when he was awake. It reached the surface of his mind from deep within his moral conscience and relentlessly accused him, "Conscienceless man! You are my murderer!" Doctors could not relieve him of these visions. In this wretched state, he finally recognized and accepted responsibility for his crime and made a full repentance. He freed all his servants and followed the dictate of his heart and conscience:

> . . . to become the humblest servant of people at the very lowest station in life. No sooner had I resolutely come to this decision than those disturbing visions of mine ceased. I felt such comfort and happiness from having made my peace with God that I cannot adequately describe it . . . the Kingdom of God is revealed in our hearts . . . leaving my native land secretly . . . for the last fifteen years I have been wandering about the whole of Siberia. Sometimes I hire myself out to the peasants for such work as I can do. Sometimes I find sustenance by begging in the name of Christ. Ah, what blessedness and what happiness and what peace of mind I enjoy in the midst of all these privations! (*The Way of a Pilgrim*, R. M. French, trans. [London, 1941], p. 112).

This true prince of the spirit bequeathed to his cherished son not riches and property but a will unlike any other. In it, he commended him to lead a spiritual life according to the wisdom he had achieved from his bitter lessons and honourable self-sacrifice to redeem his sins and purify his conscience. He wrote:

My dearest Son,

. . . In bestowing on you my paternal blessing, I adjure you to remember God and to guard your conscience. Be prudent, kindly and considerate; treat your inferiors as benevolently and amiably as you can; do not despise beggars and pilgrims, remembering that only in beggary and pilgrimage did your dying father find rest for his tormented soul. I invoke God's blessing upon you, and calmly close my eyes in the hope of life eternal, through the mercy of the Great Intercessor for men, Our Lord Jesus Christ. (Ibid., pp. 113-14)

The true source of fulfilled prayers, miracles and other extraordinary phenomena is the Divine Power immanent in all beings and inanimate matter. Everything is its conduit. Human beings are the highest instrument through which the spiritual dimension of life expresses itself. Swamiji says:

It [Raja-Yoga] declares that each man is only a conduit for the infinite ocean of knowledge and power that lies behind mankind. It teaches that desires and wants are in man, that the power of supply is also in man; and that wherever and whenever a desire, a want, a prayer has been fulfilled; it was out of this infinite magazine that the supply came, and not from any supernatural being. (*C. W.*, I: 122)

### *A SIMPLE, UNKNOWN PERSONALITY*

We find a profound spiritual conviction in humble, unheard-of personalities, whose prayerful devotion is pure and

6

simple. We would like to present the case and testimony of the miraculous healing of a Hindu devotee who wholly endowed herself to Sri Ramakrishna, Holy Mother and Guru. Nila Patel's faith in God is immaculate and bare, like a beautiful flower offering its perfume. Her acceptance of Sri Ramakrishna as God is pure and unconditional.

In 2003, Nila surrendered herself to Sri Ramakrishna during a terrible ordeal. She had to endure a series of three life-threatening brain surgeries over a five-month period. She entered the emergency room of Detroit's prestigious Henry Ford Hospital after a severe brain haemorrhage and stroke, with no hope of recovery. Part of her skull was removed, preserved at the hospital, and replaced after three months. She spent twenty-four days in the intensive care unit. Regardless of this tortured condition, she asked for nothing. She placed herself in Sri Ramakrishna's care and surrendered all her thoughts and emotions to Him. A renowned neurosurgeon, Dr. Donald M. C. Seyfried, performed Miss Patel's surgery on December 2, 2003.

Nila's story is a testament of true humility and straight-forward spiritual character. This came from her simple conviction in the full, universal redeeming grace of Sri Ramakrishna and Holy Mother Sarada Devi. These are her words:

When I opened my eyes after the first surgery, I saw next to me the picture of Sri Ramakrishna, Swami Bhuteshanandaji (my Guru) and Sri Sri Ma (Holy Mother). I had no idea of what had happened to me, except for the severe pain in my head due to the surgery. I asked a devotee, "Who brought the picture of Sri Ramakrishna?" She said, "Prasanna." I could not recollect her as I had short-term memory loss. As soon as I came out of surgery into the Intensive Care Unit, a shrine was made next to my bedside within five minutes. I looked at Sri Ramakrishna and my Guru. I remembered my Guru Mantra, and this was a start to the very slow and deliberate healing. The nurses were administering morphine round the clock and kept me sedated.

Every morning at seven o'clock, a team of neurosurgeons came to evaluate my neurological response and asked me if I knew where I was. Every morning and evening, I listened to *Arati* and *Chandi*. Somehow, I was in a different state of mind through the whole ordeal. I was calm, peaceful—I had no fear and had no questions at all. I had given myself completely to Sri Ramakrishna. I did not pray to Him to make me well. But, when the patient opposite me came out of a deep coma after twenty-one days and was able to go home, I asked Sri Ramakrishna, "When will You take me home? I want to sit in front of You in the shrine."

The nurses took excellent care of me, and pointing to Sri Ramakrishna, asked me, "Who is he?" I would tell them, "He is God and He is the Lord." I was in no state to go into details, but, since Christmas was close, I told them how Lord Jesus had merged into Him and He was also Jesus. When they asked me about Swami Bhuteshanandaji Maharaj, I told them, "He is my spiritual guide who will unite me with my Lord." At night, the nurses would relax me with a sandalwood bath and keep watch the whole night to see that I was comfortable. They would ask me why they didn't feel like leaving the room at all. Pointing at Sri Ramakrishna, I would tell them, "He is pulling you."

I always felt it was Sri Ramakrishna who was taking care of me. Once, when I was in terrible pain that was unbearable, Dr. Seyfried came at two o'clock in the morning to ask me how I was doing. He at once ordered morphine shots. All along, I felt it was Sri Ramakrishna who sent the surgeon in the middle of the night to treat me for the excruciating pain. When Dr. Seyfried had first seen me after surgery, he had said it was a miracle, since my whole brain had been covered with blood when he had first received me at the Henry Ford Hospital. I told him everybody should sing his praises for saving my life. However, it was the grace of Sri Ramakrishna that descended and He has done everything for me and to me, to make me normal. When some people had doubts as to whether I would ever be normal, I would feel like telling them, "He who has done so much to keep me and save this body—would He ever make me an invalid?"

I pray to Sri Ramakrishna every day to bring me closer and closer to Him until I merge into Him.

Niharika Patel wrote the following about her twin sister's ordeal:

My sister suffered a stroke with brain haemorrhage; her condition was very critical with 24 days in the intensive care unit. I came to help her. She is back to normal with Ma's and Thakur's grace. There were no chances of survival, as the whole brain was covered with blood when she reached the hospital, where surgery took seven hours. Part of her skull was removed and was preserved at the hospital which was replaced after three months. In five months, three brain surgeries were done. She now has a shunt which drains the spinal fluid from the brain in the pelvis. No defects are left—no complications. Neurosurgeons were concerned about her becoming blind, becoming paralyzed, etc.

In the hospital, every day, with tubes in the whole body, she performed morning and evening *Arati*. In the hospital on 16th December she repeated Holy Mother's 108 Names, offering rice at Holy Mother's feet—lying down. With Sri Ramakrishna's grace we have survived this ordeal, of course. . . . She recovered fully without any deficiency in any area. . . . I decided to attend spiritual retreats after five months of stay with my sister. I want to spend more time in spiritual practices. That too, is Thakur's will.

## ADDITIONAL BENEFITS OF TRUE PRAYER

Niharika's avowal is a poignant reminder of the additional effects of true prayer. Some of us simply cannot help praying—we find it difficult to turn away from God. Nila's testimony shows that we can cultivate this mood. At our best, we pray consciously, intelligently, devoutly and magnanimously. Our mind never outgrows prayer. We only cut ourselves off from an essential function of human life if we deny our innermost tendency to pray. Futile repetitions do not stir the soul—it is better to pray from the depth of our heart without words than to repeat exalted words that do not come from the heart. Writing on the meaning of life in his book, *The Doctor and the Soul*, Viktor Frankl observed:

There is something particularly pitiable about the man whose faith in the meaningfulness of his own existence totters in such a crisis. He has been left without moral reserves. He lacks that spiritual fire which can be supplied only by a world-view unqualifiedly affirmative towards life. Lacking this fire . . . he is unable in difficult times to 'take' the blows of fate and to set his own strength against them. He is left morally unarmed and unarmoured, prey to the full terror inherent in the concept of fate. (*The Doctor and the Soul*, p. 47)

Dr. Carrel believed "the influence of prayer on the human mind and body is as demonstrable as that of secreting glands. Its results can be measured . . . ":

> If you make a habit of sincere prayer, your life will be very noticeably and profoundly altered. Prayer stamps with its indelible mark our actions and demeanor. A tranquility of bearing, a facial and bodily repose, are observed in those whose inner lives are thus enriched. Within the depths of consciousness a flame kindles. And man sees himself. He discovers his selfishness, his silly pride, his fears, his greeds, his blunders. He develops a sense of moral obligation, intellectual humility. Thus begins a journey of the soul toward the realm of grace.
>
> Prayer is a force as real as terrestrial gravity. As a physician, I have seen men, after all other therapy has failed, lifted out of disease and melancholy by the serene effort of prayer. It is the only power in the world that seems to overcome the so-called "laws of nature"; the occasions on which prayer has dramatically done this have been termed "miracles." But a constant, quieter miracle takes place hourly in the hearts of men and women who have discovered that prayer supplies them with a steady flow of sustaining power in their daily lives.
>
> Too many people regard prayer as a formalized routine of words, a refuge for weaklings, or a childish repetition for material things. We sadly undervalue prayer when we conceive it in these terms, just as we should underestimate rain by describing it as something that fills the birdbath in our garden. Properly understood, prayer is a mature

activity indispensable to the fullest development of personality—the ultimate integration of man's highest faculties. Only in prayer do we achieve that complete and harmonious assembly of body, mind, and spirit which gives the frail human reed its unshakable strength. (Quoted from *Light from Many Lamps*, pp. 66-7)

"Be not forgetful of prayer," Dostoevsky wrote. "Every time you pray, if your prayer is sincere, there will be new feeling and new meaning in it, which will give you fresh courage and you will understand that prayer is an education." Nila's ordeal might have ended very differently, leaving her in a miserable state of mind and body. Her example of devotion and faith gives added meaning to Norman Cousins' words, "I have learnt never to underestimate the capacity of the human body to regenerate—even if the prospects seem wretched."

# 2

# THE BROAD QUESTION OF
# CULTURE AND CIVILIZATION

## A SPIRITUAL PERSPECTIVE

*There are times in the history of a man's life, nay, in the history of the lives of nations, when a sort of world-weariness becomes painfully predominant. It seems that such a tide of world-weariness has come upon the Western world. There, too, they have their thinkers, great men; and they are already finding out that this race after gold and power is all vanity of vanities; many, nay, most of the cultured men and women there, are already weary of this competition, this struggle, this brutality of their commercial civilisation, and they are looking forward towards something better. There is a class which still clings on to evils in Europe, but among the great thinkers there, other ideals are growing. They have found out that no amount of political or social manipulation of human conditions can cure the evils of life. It is a change of the soul itself for the better that alone will cure the evils of life. No amount of force, or government, or legislative cruelty will change the conditions of a race, but it is spiritual culture and ethical culture alone that can change wrong racial tendencies for the better. . . . The thoughtful men of the West find in our ancient philosophy, especially in the Vedanta, the new impulse of thought*

— 88 —

*they are seeking, the very spiritual food and drink for*
*which they are hungering and thirsting. And it is no*
*wonder that this is so.*

—Swami Vivekananda,
*Complete Works,* III: 181-2

In every nation, thoughtful men ponder the goals, aspirations and achievements or failures of civilization and culture. In common parlance, culture and civilization are interchangeable. We need to emphasize the role of culture in the development of human happiness. Our purpose is to give greater thought to the aspect of culture that adds dignity to human life. We may compare civilization, which is material, to the body, and culture, which is spiritual, to the soul. One gives happiness, the other peace. There is a strong connection between these concepts and the age-old human problem of relieving psychological, emotional, and physical stress. "Twentieth-century neurosis is the neurosis of purposelessness, valuelessness, hollowness and emptiness" (T. M. Thomas in *Images of Man: A Philosophic and Scientific Inquiry*, 1974). The modern world lacks conviction in spiritual culture, which moulds noble character. Without it, we tend to believe and trust in anything that attracts us. "When you don't have something to believe in, you will believe in everything" (G. K. Chesterton).

Popular dictionaries do not provide a true and satisfying definition of culture. In life, culture is the humanizing element. What makes us feel more affinity for one individual than for another? What enables us to approach that person willingly when some problem overwhelms us? If we seek reciprocity, authenticity and kind consideration, do we go to someone who is highly educated, fabulously successful, or famous? Do we approach the wealthiest or most politically influential individual? We approach the man or woman of simple integrity and proven ethical character, whose appealing humble nature and warm loving heart of noble compassion attract us.

Those who improve their lives by way of steadfast inner struggle to purify their mind are cultured persons. Ambition and power do not make them cultured. Capturing the essence of the sacred scriptures, they evolve by selflessly fulfiling their daily responsibilities. They are a universal soul-force for the common good with their beneficial, soothing strength.

Culture is the domain of values. "Culture" and "self-control" are synonymous. A multitude of cultured people pave the way for spiritual happiness—"as culture comes, physical happiness lessens," Swamiji says. As we lessen our attachment to physical pleasures, we give them less priority. Compassion, sympathy and consideration for others are the deeper significance of culture. These are greater than ordinary material benefits. No high culture endures without spiritual vision.

## IMPORTANT DISTINCTIONS OF CIVILIZATION AND CULTURE

The highly polarized distinctions of civilization and culture make it clear that there is a spiritual solution to stress. Civilization improves the objective world; culture elevates the subjective mind. Civilization is external and material; culture is inner and spiritual. Great civilizations possess utilitarian knowledge, civic services and material pleasures that bring worldly happiness to society; great cultures contribute to a refined humanity that enjoys vertical or spiritual growth.

Great thinkers give much importance to the development of spiritual culture. According to Plato, soul-culture "is the first and fairest thing that the best of men can ever have. Culture is born of meditation on the best that has been said and thought on the ultimate problems of life. It is the transformation of one's being." Culture is the sum of experiences, values, and symbols that society transmits from one generation to the next.

Civilization improves the objective world of nature. Mastering her secrets, we derive profit and pleasure. Culture refines, elevates and improves our condition by purifying our mind and emotions. Swami Vivekananda says:

> It is culture that withstands shocks, not a simple mass of knowledge. You can put a mass of knowledge into the world, but that will not do it much good. . . . We all know in modern times of nations which have masses of knowledge; but what of them? They are like tigers, they are like savages, because culture is not there. Knowledge is only skin-deep, as civilisation is, and a little scratch brings out the old savage. Such things happen; this is the danger. Teach the masses in the vernaculars, give them ideas; they will get information, but something more is necessary; give them culture. Until you give them that, there can be no permanence in the raised condition of the masses. (C. W., III: 291)

According to Schopenhauer, "Men are a thousand times more intent on becoming rich rather than on acquiring culture, though it is quite certain that what a man is, contributes more to his happiness than what he has." The true nature of the intellect is spiritual. A spiritually oriented mind alone makes us happy, peaceful and enlightened and brings stability to society.

We cannot afford to ignore the basic logic behind the maxim, "What we think we become." We strengthen our inner qualities through a spiritual orientation to life. This is the highest perception of social structure, which unites culture and civilization. British historian Arnold Toynbee (1889-1975) remarked, "Seeking God is itself a social act." A genuine spiritual person invariably sets the example of a noble life.

Becoming aware of the timeless Hindu values enables us to cultivate happiness spiritually. They include firm faith in the following principles: (1) our divine heritage; (2) unity of existence; (3) freedom of conscience in religion; (4) sacredness of life; (5) sanctity of family life; (6) respect for parents and elders and reverence for the spiritual teacher; (7) the Motherhood of God; (8) moderate pursuit of material welfare; (9) steadfast pursuit of "self-integration and Self-realization" and (10) renunciation and service for the good of the common people.

High civilization and high culture meet in the Preamble of the UNESCO's Constitution. To support its basic premise, the UNESCO erected four pillars of education through which society is to promote worldwide peace and harmony: "learning to learn," "learning to do," "learning to be," and "learning to live with others." The first pillar is a vital prerequisite for a complete education.

According to a noted social thinker, "Educators are guilty of violence when they tell students that they have no free soul but are passionate creatures. To be a victim of intellectual robbers who despoil man of his Divine image is to create the gravest social problems." Alfred North Whitehead defined education as "the acquisition of the art of the utilization of knowledge." A distinguished former president of Columbia University called the popular misconceptions of education "the three errors." He maintains, "The first is to suppose that the main purpose of school is to train boys and girls to be sociable. The second is that education ends when leaving school. The third is to suppose that learning ought to show profit or lead to success" (Gilbert Highet, *Man's Unconquerable Mind* [New York, 1954], pp. 75ff).

Carl Jung notes the damaging effects of these "errors":

> The wine of youth does not always clear with advancing years; oftentimes it grows turbid. . . . The neurotic is rather a person who can never have things as he would like them in the present, and who can therefore never enjoy the past. (*Modern Man in Search of a Soul*, p. 108)

Many intelligent, cultivated people make the rude discovery in middle age that they have not prepared themselves to live meaningfully in the first half or "morning" of life—they have no real foundation. According to Jung, "For the most part our old people try to compete with the young. In the United States it is almost an ideal for the father to be the brother of his sons, and for the mother if possible to be the younger sister of her daughter" (*Modern Man in Search of a Soul*, p. 126). The "morning" of life refers to nature, which leads us to external pursuits and goals. The worldly values that brought them economic, professional, intellectual and material satisfaction have not brought them deeper, lasting satisfaction and hope:

> Wholly unprepared, they embark upon the second half of life. Or are there perhaps colleges for forty-year-olds which prepare them for their coming life and its demands as the ordinary colleges introduce our young people to a knowledge of the world and of life? No, there are none. Thoroughly unprepared we take the step into the afternoon of life; worse still, we take this step with the false presupposition that our truths and ideals will serve us as hitherto. . . . Our religions were always such schools in the past, but how many people regard them as such today?

How many of us older persons have really been . . . prepared for the second half of life, for old age, death and eternity? (*Modern Man in Search of a Soul*, pp. 108-9)

The "afternoon" of a spiritually cultivated existence leads to a fulfilling inner life guided by spiritual purpose. The common problems of melancholia and depression that plague many elderly people do not exist for such a person:

> The best insurance against melancholia, depression, and a sense of futility in old age is the development of wide horizons and the cultivation of mental elasticity and interest in the world. Unlike the flesh, the spirit does not decay with the years. Many of the happiest individuals in the world are men and women in their sixties, seventies, or eighties, who have contributed richly to the world's work during their maturity, and at the same time have cultivated sufficient awareness and interest in the undying cultural activities to make their leisure a delight. . . . The older men grow the more they realize that it is only by putting the focus of their activities in some movement or activity greater than their individual ego, that they can attain peace and security in old age. (W. Beran Wolfe)

Jung says that the goal of culture transcends the mere satisfaction of natural requirements:

> . . . The afternoon of human life must also have a significance of its own and cannot be merely a pitiful appendage to life's morning. The significance of the morning undoubtedly lies in the development of the individual, our entrenchment in the outer world, the propagation of our kind and the care of our children. This is the obvious purpose of nature. But when this purpose has been attained—and even more than attained—shall the

earning of money, the extension of conquests and the expansion of life go steadily on beyond the bounds of all reason and sense? Whoever carries over into the afternoon the law of the morning—that is, the aims of nature—must pay for doing so with damage to his soul just as surely as a growing youth who tries to salvage his childish egoism must pay for this mistake with social failure. Money-making, social existence, family, posterity are nothing but plain nature—not culture. Culture lies beyond the purpose of nature" (*Modern Man in Search of a Soul*, pp. 109-110).

Spiritual culture takes into account the life-saving rules of conduct that inhibit or remove evil tendencies and foster spiritual growth. When we apply spiritual principles to everything we think and do, we increase the "quality, quantity and intensity" of our lives. "People become rich, not by saving, but by working and making the money they have earned work instead of lying idle. Not to hate one's neighbor is good, but to love him is far better" (Alexis Carrel, *Reflections on Life*, p. 92). Swamiji says that an improved quality of life makes human beings humane:

> We are always losing sight of the real meaning of things. The little eating and dress! Every fool can see that. Who sees that which is beyond? It is culture of the heart that we want. (*C. W.*, IV: 222)

It is one of the evils of your Western civilisation that you are after intellectual education alone, and take no care of the heart. It only makes men ten times more selfish, and that will be your destruction. . . . Intellect can never become inspired; only the heart, when it is enlightened, becomes inspired. An intellectual, heartless man never becomes an inspired man. . . . Intellect has been cultured, with the result that hundreds of sciences have been discovered, and their effect has been that the few have made slaves of the many—that is all the good that has been done. Artificial wants have been created and every poor man, whether he has money or not, desires to have those wants satisfied; and when he cannot, he struggles, and dies in the struggle. This is the result. Through the intellect is not the way to solve the problem of misery, but through the heart. If all this vast amount of effort had been spent in making men purer, gentler, more forbearing, this world would have a thousandfold more happiness than it has today. (*C. W.*, I: 412-15)

Love combined with wisdom preserves life; it does not destroy it. A civilized world without spiritual principles hinders life with deeds far worse than manslaughter:

The profiteer who sends up the price of necessities, the financier who cheats poor people of their savings, the industrialist who does not protect his workmen against poisonous substances . . . are all murderers. (*Reflections on Life*, p. 92-3)

Family abuse, uninspired education that ignores morality and ethics, and high suicide rates in the young and elderly are additional harmful effects.

In his essay, "The Gospel of Relaxation," Williams James wrote, "The American overtension and jerkiness and breathlessness and intensity and agony of expression . . . are *bad habits,* nothing more or less" (Quoted from Dale Carnegie, *How to Stop Worrying and Start Living* [New York, 1985], p. 239). Dr. Carrel also pinpointed the issue: we destroy the spiritual self through "all those thoughts, acts and habits which tend to lower our vitality, to disturb the balance of our nervous systems or our minds, to cause disease or to diminish the quality and length of our lives" (*Reflections on Life*, p. 93). His words, first recorded in 1960, are eternally relevant and deserve our notice:

To preserve life, it is not enough to refrain from destroying it. We must also make it wider, deeper, bolder, and more joyful. Strength is the only thing which allows man to rise higher . . . The strength we need does not resemble the muscular strength of the athlete, the moral strength of the ascetic or the intellectual strength of the philosopher and the scientist. It comprises stamina, harmony, and suppleness of muscles, organs and mind along with the capacity to bear fatigue, hunger, sorrow, and anxiety. It is the will and the hope to act; the solidarity of the body and the soul which does not admit the possibility of defeat: the joy which permeates our whole being.

How can we acquire this strength? The only way is by patient, dogged effort; unconscious effort on the part of the heart, the glands and all the anatomical system; conscious effort on the part of the will, the intelligence and the muscles. One must learn, little by little, by exercises repeated every day, to establish order in one's life, to accept one's self-imposed discipline and to be one's own master. One must also train oneself, by small and frequent efforts, to dominate one's feelings, one's nervousness, pride, laziness, and suffering. Such an apprenticeship is indispensable to any civilized person; the basic error of modern teaching is to have neglected it. (*Reflections on Life*, p. 95)

We improve our moral foundation by creating, implementing, fostering and upholding non-dogmatic principles that reflect higher values. This demonstrates that a high civilization imbued with spiritual principles is the highest meeting-place of civilization and culture in a mature society.

We expect any mature society to value the higher purpose of Nature, which creates and nurtures us. If we are self-centred, pleasure-seeking, aimless, rootless and selfish, Nature, whose purpose is never fulfilled by living irresponsibly without ethics, becomes our nemesis. Pitirim Sorokin says:

> Civilized societies, which have most strictly limited sexual freedom have developed the highest culture. In the whole of human history not a single case is found in which a society has been able to advance to the Rationalistic Culture without its women being born and reared in a rigidly enforced pattern of faithfulness to one man. Further, there is no example of a community, which has retained its high position on the culture scale after less rigorous sexual customs have replaced more restricting ones. (Pitirim Sorokin, *Sane Sex Order* [Bharatiya Vidya Bhavan, 1961], p. 38)

The civilized world admires Arnold Toynbee for his painstaking research of twenty-one civilizations extended over forty years (1921 to 1961). We find in his twelve volumes of *A Study of History* an exhaustive survey and analysis of human development wherever humanity adhered to ethical, moral and religious principles. With his characteristic unified perspective he wrote, "A civilization, rather than the traditional nation states, ought to be the unit for the study of history." Toynbee proposed that civilizations perish from within. He claimed that degraded moral culture, not political invasions, destroyed nineteen of the twenty-one world civilizations he studied. Therefore he believed, "Morals cannot stand on their own feet, but must be based on religion. We cannot make new religions in cold blood but must stick to traditional religions, clearing out non-essential accretions."

Vivekananda defined civilization as "a manifestation of divinity in man" and says that "God is to religion what Newton's law of gravity is to falling bodies." Religion is what we do in our solitariness. Seekers of truth seek the hidden soul-force, the animating inner power that sustains and invigorates us. Religion binds us to our source. Gordon Allport says:

> Religion is the search for a value underlying ALL things, and as such is the most comprehensive of all the possible philosophies of life. A deeply moving religious experience is not readily forgotten, but is likely to remain as a focus of thought and desire. (Gordon W. Allport, *Personality, A Psychological Interpretation* [New York, 1937], p. 226)

Dag Hammarskjöld once remarked, "On this bookshelf of life, God is a useful book of reference, always at hand but seldom consulted." Mahatma Gandhi constantly referred to "The Great Book." From a tender age, he understood the impact of truth on the culture of well-being. The "General Knowledge" section of his matriculation examination in London included the question, "What is more golden than gold?" He answered, "Truth is more golden than gold." Gandhiji's life is an open book of a truth-seeker's success in developing integrity of character. All young people in their formative years will profit immensely if they are introduced to his autobiography. Reading it may prevent them from falling headlong into the abyss of sensate culture.

## SPIRITUAL DIMENSION OF LIFE

We need to practise spiritual values because they destroy the root cause of suffering. "A society corrupted by love of money and by spiritual emptiness . . . has every sort of possession except self-possession, and every sort of security except a social order founded on the essential nature of man: above all, his capacity for love and sacrifice" (Lewis Mumford, *Faith for Living*, [New York, 1940], pp. 226-7). Before the Great Depression of the 1930s, many of the world's great financiers proudly displayed their wealth and power. They possessed fame and prestige, intelligence, education, glamour and excitement. The Great Depression brought a humiliating, penniless death to many of them; some committed suicide. They lacked faith in the underlying spiritual dimension of life, which is everywhere in nature but remains largely unperceived. "For those who seek it, there is inexhaustible evidence of an all-pervading intelligence."

Admiral Richard E. Byrd could well have contemplated suicide, living frozen and alone in a tiny shack for five months in the Antarctic winter of 1934. One day when he was working in the icy cold, gathering scientific data, something made him hesitate before returning to his shack. Standing still, he gazed at the ice, listening deeply to the intense stillness of its vast expanse. He experienced a profound sense of oneness with the rhythm of the universe and felt an inner awakening of tremendous faith. "I am not alone," he thought. "The human voice is not alone in the universe." Remarkably, he felt pervaded by warmth in "the coldest cold on the face of the earth." To his scientific and personal record of that research project, he gave the title, *Alone*, and wrote:

> The conviction came that that rhythm was too orderly, too harmonious, too perfect to be a product of blind chance—that, therefore, there must be purpose in the whole and that man was part of that whole and not an accidental offshoot. It was a feeling that transcended reason; that

went to the heart of a man's despair and found it groundless. The universe was a cosmos, not a chaos; man was as rightfully a part of that cosmos as were the day and night. (Quoted from *Light from Many Lamps*, p. 34)

He gained another conviction: "Half the confusion in the world comes from not knowing how little we need. . . . I live more simply now, and with more peace" (Ibid., p. 237).

"The heavens declare the glory of God; and the firmament showeth his handiwork" (*Psalm* 19:1). "I cannot conceive," said Abraham Lincoln, "how a man could look up into the heavens and say there is no God." Contemplating nature, we feel oneness with the universe. It addresses the heart of our despair, of our suffering and egoism and reveals them to be baseless. According to Ralph Waldo Emerson:

> If the stars should appear one night in a thousand years, how men would believe and adore, and preserve for many generations the remembrance of the City of God which had been shown! But every night come out these envoys of beauty, and light the universe with their admonishing smile . . . In the woods we return to reason and faith. Standing on the bare ground—my head bathed by the blithe air, and uplifted into infinite space—all mean egotism vanishes. . . . The currents of the Universal Being circulate through me. (Quoted from *Light from Many Lamps*, p. 35)

"But for even the humblest person," Mumford wrote, "a day spent without the sight or sound of beauty, the contemplation of mystery or the search for truth and perfection, is a poverty-stricken day; a succession of such days is fatal in human life." Society is morally deficient. Aside from going to places of worship, many people try to get their spiritual values from psychotherapy. To alleviate their anxiety, many resort to medicines and at the very worst, to hallucinogenic drugs. They have lost the naturally wholesome and spiritual order of life. In an age of unprecedented swift access to information, vast numbers of men, women and children are addicted to the internet. They are directed away from their best interests by their lack of discrimination and spiritual values. Their various compulsive disorders mask a genuine and occasionally desperate search for the spiritual meaning of life.

Ignorance of the Self or Soul is the root cause of all our suffering. If we feel defeated and cheated in life, it is due to our wrong perspective. A trace of unspiritual emotion can generate its more stubborn and resistant forms: intense jealousy, hatred, envy, fear, anger, insecurity, uncertainty, depression and anxiety. Adhering to a spiritual perspective prepares us to develop our Soul-consciousness.

The spiritual dimension of life gives knowledge of the Self. This is the authentic meaning of "culture." If the mind remains on the lower sensate planes, we can never be happy anywhere. The more we dwell on matter, the more material we become; the more we dwell on the Divine, the more divine we become. We must improve the spiritual quality of the mind.

## ADDRESSING THE PROBLEMS OF SECULAR CULTURE

Society today pays a heavy price for its reprehensible secular values and achievements. "Never before was man so dedicated, yet so ignorant; so profusely equipped, yet so insecure; so much in plenty, yet in such penury; and so highly civilized, yet morally so low." We should be asking ourselves, "What have we become, what are we?" not, "What have we achieved?" Jung accurately says, "Achievement, usefulness and so forth—

are the ideals which appear to guide us out of the confusion of crowding problems . . . They may help us in striking our roots in the world; but they cannot guide us in the development of that wider consciousness to which we give the name of culture" (*Modern Man in Search of a Soul*, p. 103).

## NERVOUS AND MENTAL DISORDERS

Industrialization stifles our naturally healthy instincts. The by-products of development and large municipalities—pollution, long, unsafe job commutes, cold, grey streets, grimy conditions and selfish indifference of people rushing to and fro—wear down most city dwellers. It is not surprising that almost everyone who lives in an industrial society suffers a bout or two of nervous fatigue and knows someone who has had a nervous breakdown. Corporate executives and other professionals are especially prone to these conditions.

Industrialization has steered us to "abnormal pressure all the time—from noise, pollution, negative emotions, improper diet, smoking, alcohol, and so on . . .[introducing] the new 'disease of being in a hurry'" (Deepak Chopra, M. D., *Quantum Healing* [New York, 1990], p. 193). We are convinced that we have no time to relax and reassess our goals in life. We are victimized by an artificial "need" to work on which we lay the blame for our nervous condition—"I reacted suddenly to my heavy work schedule," we rationalize to our doctor and friends. Too much work is not the cause of the breakdown. Some intolerable emotional problem or misfortune that made us seek escape through work is usually lurking behind our breakdown. The well-known Metropolitan Life Insurance Company once printed a leaflet on fatigue that read, "Hard work by itself seldom causes fatigue which cannot be cured by a good sleep or rest. . . . Worry, tenseness, and emotional upsets are three of the biggest causes of fatigue" (Quoted from *How to Stop Worrying and Start Living*, p. 238).

Fatigue brings on premature aging. According to Dr. Deepak Chopra, premature aging is a condition we no longer question and have come to expect as an "inevitable aspect of normal life . . . Some people live longer than others owing to privileged genes, a strong immune system, or good luck, but there is no anti-aging factor that can be applied to everyone" (*Quantum Healing*, p. 193). Fascinated with the implications of this problem, Dr. Robert Keith Wallace (known for his validating research for over a decade on the effects of Transcendental Meditation on the mind and body) investigated its effects on the aging process. He tested three variables that are convenient markers of biological age in adults practising TM: blood pressure, hearing capacity and near-sightedness. They all deteriorate with age. The meditators proved to be biologically younger than their chronological age—one of them fully twenty years younger. Wallace was able to show a positive correlation between years of meditation practice and youthfulness. The onset of this correlation begins with five years' meditation practice. Age is not a variable, since the positive correlation of meditation and looking younger than one's years occurred in older as well as younger subjects (*Quantum Healing*, p. 194).

The real cause of mental and nervous disorders, the lack of healthy values and the supreme spiritual goal, eludes everyone. "Psychoneurosis must be understood as the suffering of a human being who has not discovered what life means to him" (Jung). Lacking a self-image founded on spiritual truths, we flounder in a sea of action, unclear about our direction. We are without will power, which derives from a clear knowledge of the Self. Psychologist Dr. Maxwell Maltz wrote: "All your action, feelings, behavior, even your abilities are always consistent with this self-image. In short, you will act like the sort of person you conceive yourself to be. Not only this, but you literally cannot act otherwise in spite of your conscious efforts or will power" (Maxwell Maltz, M. D., *Psycho-cybernetics: A New Way to Get More Living Out of Life* [New York, 1960] Quoted from *Gospel of the Life Sublime, Vol. I*, p. 172).

Spiritual values protect us from unbridled emotional reactions to problems and misfortunes, and from an unsteady, confused mind unable to think clearly. A serene mind made peaceful through mental discipline cures nervous conditions that prevent our progress. A serene mind indicates a spiritual orientation to life.

## "PSYCHOSURGERY"

Today, physicians and patients alike look to medicines and surgical neurological procedures of clinically proven, swift efficiency in the central nervous system. Psychotropic medicines chemically subdue the emotions or destroy the unpleasant effects of neurosis, depression and anxiety. However, they have no permanent effect on their root cause. The practice of lobotomy, one of the most glaring surgical "quick fix" attempts to relieve countless sufferers, began in the mid-twentieth century.

Lobotomy severs the nerve fibers of the two frontal lobes of the brain. It was invented by neuropsychiatry's Dr. Antonio de Egas Moniz of Portugal to reduce the effects of severe mental disorders (Henry C. Link, *The Rediscovery of Man*, p. 93). Dr. Moniz performed the first lobotomy, popularly known as "psychicsurgery," on a human patient in 1935. His initial twenty-one hour-long operations caused such severe behaviour disorders in patients that the Portuguese government forbade further lobotomies. In 1949, Dr. Moniz received the Nobel

Prize in medicine for his discovery of this procedure as an effective remedy for certain specific psychoses. Ironically, one of his allegedly successful lobotomy patients became insane and shot him, leaving him with a bullet in the spine, which entirely paralyzed one side of his body.

In Washington, D. C., neurologist Dr. Walter Freeman shortened the length of the procedure by applying powerful electric shocks to induce the coma state required for surgery more quickly. Lobotomies were then performed within ten minutes in a doctor's office. He supervised 4,000 lobotomies and his promotion of them through lectures and writings make him potentially accountable for 20,000 more. Doctors continued to utilize this drastic form of surgery to bring relief to patients suffering from schizophrenia, neurosis, depression, anxiety and suicidal tendencies. Between 1936 and 1956, almost 50,000 Americans were lobotomized.

One essayist called it "murder of the mind." The frontal lobes encompass the emotional, reasoning, insight, judgement, empathy and self-awareness faculties of the human mind that distinguish us from other creatures whose nature is instinctive. Severing the nerve fibers of the frontal lobes severs the individual from the highest faculties of spiritual potentiality of the mind. Though it allows patients to live and brings mental relief to some, lobotomy deprives them of spiritual development.

Patients often turn to some form of psychiatric help in addition to this form of treatment. Psychotherapy does not permanently solve problems and poses yet another: the strong possibility that the therapist may impose his views and principles upon the vulnerable patient who is seeking a cure. The fact that man is essentially spiritual continues to go largely unnoticed by the psychiatric community. It persists in the worldly premise that we are material beings comprising body, mind and emotions. For many therapists, the soul is either non-existent or separate; therapists rarely consider it a crucial element of therapy:

> One of the great tragedies of our times is that atheistic humanists have so brainwashed our culture into thinking that man is an animal without a spiritual dimension to life that most people possess few spiritual reserves upon which to draw in times of mental, emotional, or physical distress. Instead, the giant God-void within them seriously compounds their problems and hampers recovery. (Dr. Tim LaHaye, *How to Win Over Depression*, 1976, p. 62)

The limited success of the radical treatments of electric shock therapy, lobotomy, and the common use of psychotropic drugs to deal with anxiety, depression and neurosis, indicates that something additional is required for lasting beneficial effects. "Neurosis, it now appears, is not the result of biological frustration but of moral frustration" (Prof. Mowrer). We need clear, deeply felt ideals to live by. Neurosis is guided by the demands of the ego, which seeks to assert itself over others. "Every neurosis can be understood as an attempt to free oneself from a feeling of inferiority in order to gain a feeling of superiority" (Alfred Adler).

### STATE OF WAR AGAINST THE SELF

Jung says, "Neurosis is an inner cleavage—the state of being at war with oneself. Everything that accentuates this cleavage makes the patient worse, and everything that mitigates it tends to heal the patient. What drives people to war with themselves is the intuition or the knowledge that they consist of two persons in opposition to one another. . . A neurosis is a dissociation of personality" (*Modern Man in Search of a Soul*, pp. 236-7).

Untreated neurosis eventually enslaves the entire personality, which is no longer able to reason or act appropriately. To escape from the grip of neurosis, the entire personality must come under treatment and be guided by higher ideals. Significantly, a healthy sense of detachment helps us in every sphere of life. Ancient Greek playwrights sometimes deliberately added comedy to their tragedies in order to provide us with a sense of detachment from the awful realities of human tragedy as well as emotional purification.

From its mildest to its most severe forms, depression is universal—no one is exempt from it at one time or another. Many factors contribute to depression: inability to accept illness and death, ambivalence about important events, extreme disappointment and rejection. Poor self-esteem due to our lack of conviction in the divinity of life, a restless mind and lack of a spiritual goal are factors that are more serious. Our frame of reference is material and self-serving; it is not spiritual and self-abnegating. Without a spirit of accommodation, we will always be prone to anger and self-pity as soon as we perceive our lack of self-fulfilment. Sri Ramakrishna says, "Anger arises when obstacles are placed in the way of desire" (*Gospel*, p. 247).

Depression is a condition of profound ignorance regarding the purpose of life. It shows a lack of balance in the daily flow of give-and-take in life. "The self-life always causes depression," says one Christian counsellor who advises that "Making Christ [the] Lord of your life each day enables you to avoid self-pity, self-indulgence, self-centeredness, and the many natural expressions of selfishness" (*How to Win Over Depression*, p. 189).

## SELF-FORGETFULNESS, HEALTH AND HAPPINESS

Depression can be minor and brief or chronic and lasting. On the other hand, it may be such a major obstacle to our mental, emotional, psychological and physical stability that it paralyzes us spiritually and even threatens life. Remarkably, some people who find themselves in this condition are able to "forget themselves into health and happiness." Dr. Frederic Loomis lived to serve and devote himself to others. From his deathbed, he pondered upon George Eliot's lines, "It's but little good you'll do, watering last year's crops." Aroused from his lethargy, he began to write *The Best Medicine*, possibly the most significant article of his life:

> *It's but little good you'll do, watering last year's crops.* Yet that is exactly what I have seen hundreds of my patients doing in the past twenty-five years—watering with freely-flowing tears things of the irrevocable past. . . . Moaning over what cannot be helped is a confession of futility and fear, of emotional stagnation—in fact, of selfishness and cowardice. The best way to break this vicious, morbid circle—"to snap out of it"—is to stop thinking about yourself, and start thinking about other people. You can lighten your own load by doing something for someone else. By the simple device of doing an outward, unselfish act today, you can make the past recede. The present and future will take on their true challenge and perspective.
>
> As a doctor, I have seen it many, many times and nearly always, it has been a far more successful prescription than anything I could have ordered from the drugstore. (Quoted from *Light from Many Lamps*, p. 223-4)

He left these inspiring words as he lay dying: "Stop thinking about yourself . . .lighten your own load by doing something for someone else . . . it will keep you from morbid worry and fears . . . it's the best medicine" (Ibid., p. 224).

The ideal of selfless service also came to the popular novelist Margaret Taylor Yates during World War II. Japan's bombs struck Pearl Harbour and left 2,117 people dead and 960 missing. For over a year before the bombing, she had been confining herself to bed twenty-two hours a day, after being diagnosed with heart disease. She felt like a complete invalid, defeated physically and emotionally, and expected to spend the rest of her life in that condition with others waiting on her. Her extreme body-consciousness had worn her out. After the bombing however, a new and inspiring thought arose within her. The misery and plight of more unfortunate people than herself awakened a need in her to serve them and alleviate their pain. It jarred her out of her despondency and for a significant period, she was no longer preoccupied with her body.

When the Red Cross asked for assistance, she immediately volunteered and firmly planted herself in service. They appointed her a telephone liaison, to relay vital information between Army and Navy staff members and their families, who had to live temporarily in public schools and private homes. Besides providing a vital refuge from fear and chaos, her home was an efficient clearinghouse of information serving the nation's security interests. While liaising, she was relieved and grateful to learn that her husband, Commander Raleigh Yates was safe after the invasion.

She also discovered her great inner capacity for selfless service. She consoled many widows. At first, Mrs. Yates worked from the phone next to her bed, but soon forgot her own weakness completely and shifted first to a table and then to a chair. She never returned to her habit of staying in bed. "The attack on Pearl Harbour was one of the greatest tragedies in

American history," she confessed, "but as far as I was concerned, it was one of the best things that ever happened to me. That terrible crisis gave me strength that I never dreamed I possessed. It took my attention off myself and focused it on others. It gave me something big and vital and important to live for. I no longer had time to think about myself or care about myself" (Quoted from *How to Stop Worrying and Start Living*, pp. 178-180 passim). In almost every society, we find that critical emergencies bring out the inner strength of its citizens.

In another case, a sixty-year-old woman diagnosed with incurable manic-depression, also found happiness through self-forgetfulness. She had been prone to severe, lengthy spells of depression for years. Costly travels for a change of scene that her psychiatrists prescribed brought her minimal relief. She got away from her home but not from her mental troubles, which accompanied her wherever she went. Though highly educated, cultured, healthy and strong, she was selfishly absorbed in resentments. Her lifestyle was sedentary and insular with few friends. She had to take care of her elder sister who lived with her. Though she had worked over thirty years in a bank, she knew nothing about her colleagues. When she learned to focus her thoughts and develop her insight, she thought less about herself and more about the needs and concerns of others around her. She became convinced that it was more effective to give happiness to others than to indulge herself. When she became established in selflessness, it made her soul happy. Her spiritual joy cured her depression (*The Rediscovery of Man*, pp. 98-9).

## THE QUESTION OF BLAME

Self-pity and self-absorption often lead to blame of others or oneself. We should drop blame from our thought and speech. Swamiji says, "Our thoughts, our words and deeds are the threads of the net which we throw round ourselves, for good or for evil. Once we set in motion a certain power, we have to take the full consequences of it." Again, "These results condition the life of man. Thus he moulds his own life. Man is not bound by any other laws excepting those which he makes for himself" (*C. W.*, II: 348). We create our own fate.

The morbid habit of laying blame on others deprives us of a spiritual perspective and the ability to forgive. It stifles our ability to love and feel compassion for others. If we accept and forgive others, we are freed from the blaming habit. "For if you forgive men their trespasses, your heavenly Father also will forgive you; but if you do not forgive men their trespasses, neither will your Father forgive your trespasses" (Matthew 6:14-15). Forgiving is so important that Christ says, "I do not say to you seven times, but seventy times seven" (Matthew 18:22).

Turning our thoughts to God relieves our heart of the oppressive spiritual, mental and emotional guilt of an unforgiving spirit. We receive inspiration to reject selfish tendencies and follow the higher spiritual and moral teachings of the Holy Ones.

## "YOUR REAL TIE IS WITH GOD"
## A SPIRITUAL APPROACH

Sri Ramakrishna says, "Repeat His name, and sins will disappear. Thus you will destroy lust, anger, the desire for creature comforts and so on" (*Gospel*, p. 203). Whether or not God is currently in vogue, the fact remains that a person centred in spirituality and selflessness is capable of controlling depression and its powerful elemental forces of selfishness and anger. Until we recognize that depression and anger are signs of spiritual ignorance and stop all our attempts to justify them, our plight will be hopeless. Hopelessness and anger make us "spiritual pigmies." To reduce these universally domineering emotions, we need to practise "the peace of God, which passeth all understanding" (Phil. 4:7). Practising the peace of God means to become aware of the spiritual essence immanent in life.

We can surrender to God through inward prayer and seek His grace by making Him the "attorney" who resolves all our grievances. Because this highest form of worship brings relief, God gives this teaching in every living scripture. Yet we continue to reject God and Godliness and increase our dependency on the external aids of psychotropic medications and counselling, or we sink into the depraved state of illicit drug use and other degenerate forms of escapism.

We need, instead, to increase our worship. Harbouring impure thoughts in the mind is not a conducive attitude to worship. He worships truly whose heart is pure and loving, whose conscience is clear and unburdened. Therefore, Christ tells us not to worship in the temple until we have settled our disputes and made peace with anyone towards whom we have ill feelings. He commands us to forgive and release our anger as quickly as possible before our worship. "Let not the sun go down upon your wrath" (Eph. 4:26).

Sri Ramakrishna says, "One receives the grace of God by subduing the passions—lust, anger and greed" (*Gospel*, p. 161). We can humbly surrender to God the strong emotions that come from our displeasure. We can pray, "O Lord, even as you can transform life, I ask you to please transform me. Please bring my passions under Your control."

When we subdue our nature, or ego, and become peaceful, anger dissipates and vanishes, leaving our mind purified. "Muddied water let stand, will become clear" (Lao-tse). How can the shackles of mounting resentment, irritation, anger

8

and hatred be broken? We must fill our mind with the opposing attitudes of forgiveness, faith and love and avoid provocation. We will be blessed with purity and vitality. "Blessed are the pure in heart: for they shall see God" (Matthew 5:8).

Holy Mother says, "My child, don't be worried. These earthly ties are transitory. Today they seem to be the be-all and end-all of life and tomorrow they vanish. Your real tie is with God" (*Thus Spake The Holy Mother*, p. 84). Repeating God's Name, the Mantra, or any sacred verse or prayer reduces the power of anger and depression in the mind and their unhealthy physical effects. *Japa* of the Mantra is a particularly powerful aid. Swami Brahmananda would tell his disciples:

> Plunge yourself deep into the practice of Japa and meditation. Now the mind is gross and feeds on gross objects. But as Japa and meditation are practised, the mind becomes subtle and learns to grasp subtle truths. Practise, practise. See for yourself if there really is a God. . . . The veils of Maya will be removed one after another; a new vision will open. Then you will see what a wonderful treasure lies within you. You will unfold your own divinity and inherit eternal happiness. (*The Eternal Companion*, pp. 164, 165)

The power of God's Name makes itself felt mysteriously. Constant repetition of the holy Name with *Om* purifies the mind and heart and counteracts negative thoughts. In his *Yoga Sutras* (I: 27, 28) Patanjali says:

> After the repetition of OM, the spiritual seeker should have recourse to meditation; after meditation he should again take to repetition. Through the perfection of repetition and meditation, the Supreme Spirit becomes

manifest. . . . All the obstacles cease to exist by virtue of devotion to the Lord, and then follows for him the perception of his own real nature. He comes to realize that just as the Lord is Spirit—pure, blissful, free from troubles—so also is the spirit which functions through the mind. (Quoted from *Adventures in Vedanta*, p. 117)

The purified body and mind possess a spiritual vibration. The divine Name removes all obstacles, uplifts the soul and unites it with God. "He who walks in darkness, to whom no light appears, let him trust in the name of Yahweh, let him rely upon his God" (Isaiah 50:10). Mahatma Gandhi, a votary of *Ramanama*, realized the spiritual benefit of *Japa* in his life and in his dying breath. Impure urges, instincts and passions in the mind make it waver, and rob it of peacefulness. In his *Yoga Sutras* (I: 33) Patanjali says, "Undisturbed calmness of mind is attained by cultivating (1) friendliness towards the happy, (2) compassion for the unhappy, (3) delight in the good, and (4) indifference to the evil." Swamiji says:

> We must have these four sorts of ideas. We must have friendship for all; we must be merciful towards those that are in misery; when people are happy, we ought to be happy; and to the wicked we must be indifferent. So with all subjects that come before us. If the subject is a good one, we shall feel friendly towards it; if the subject of thought is one that is miserable, we must be merciful towards it. (*C. W.*, I: 222)

Rarely do we find a calm, self-composed and mature person whose gentle response increases our anger. Rarer still is the self-restrained, enlightened person who can be provoked to react and can be incited to violence of any kind. His peaceful presence transforms banal anger into sublime peacefulness.

If we cannot follow the rigour of a purely spiritual approach or emulate the example of holy persons, we can at least try to fix our mind on spiritual thoughts and higher ideals whenever we realize that lower thoughts have grabbed our attention. Every time we do this, we create a strong link of resistance to the illusory power of Maya, which plays on all the emotions. There are many practical suggestions besides.

## PRACTICAL APPROACHES TO ANGER

*Webster's Dictionary* provides the related synonyms of the word, *anger*: "*Anger* is broadly applicable to feelings of resentful or revengeful displeasure; *indignation* implies righteous anger aroused by what seems unjust; mean, or insulting; *rage* suggests a violent outburst of anger in which self-control is lost; *fury* implies a frenzied rage that borders on madness; *ire*, chiefly a literary word, suggests a show of great anger in acts, words, looks, etc.; *wrath* implies deep indignation expressing itself in a desire to punish or get revenge."

Anger is hard to control; extreme, uncontrolled anger can lead to acts of insanity. Ordinary anger has many ill effects—it provokes high blood pressure, rapid breathing and raging pulse. It is self-defeating to wallow in unconstructive, irritating emotions, which often lead to serious illness. In his article, "Heart-to-Heart Advice about Heart Trouble," San Francisco physician Dr. Charles Miner Cooper wrote, "You must curb your emotional reactions. When I tell you that I have known a patient's blood pressure to jump sixty points almost instantaneously in response to an outburst of anger, you can understand what strain such reactions throw upon the heart" (Quoted from Norman Vincent Peale, *The Power of Positive Thinking* [Delhi, 1975], p. 210).

Due to anger, we may commit violence against ourselves or other beings, creatures and objects. Our temporary lapse and fearful appearance threaten others who may seek to avoid us or to respond defensively with aggression. Worst of all, anger makes us feel isolated and separated from God, our eternal Well-wisher and Friend. Anger is definitely a temporary form of insanity.

If we can resolve our grievances and the likelihood of anger when they first appear, we can prevent their distortion at the outset. Sometimes, simply unburdening our complaints to a sympathetic trusted person eliminates them. However, if we have to take a more positive approach, certain practical techniques are very effective. First, we can make a list of irritations before they add up and increase their power in the mind. Success does not come overnight. The thought that, "If men are so wicked with religion, what would they be without it?" made a strong impression on Benjamin Franklin. For many years, he recorded his failings every day in his diary and measured his steady progress.

Second, we can add prayer to self-discipline, which increases our moral strength. We easily reduce the strength of irritations, one at a time, through prayer. The "spiritual iodine" of forbearance, love and forgiveness on anger's wounds together with sincere prayer makes the remedy permanent.

Third, we can oppose anger with reason. Anger is foolish, futile and improbable in sober people with spiritual discrimination. Sri Ramakrishna says, "Reason, by all means, about the Real and the Unreal, about what is permanent and what is transitory. You must reason when you are overcome by lust, anger, or grief" (*Gospel*, p. 496). If we review our experience with anger and observe life but a little, we will immediately realize that anger has never given us emotional stability and peace of mind. It does not resolve differences harmoniously. Faith in the faculty of reason develops will power; a resolute mind supports reason. Reason and will power combined strongly oppose anger.

Fourth, we can make a strong display of harmless disapproval to ward off danger if we feel threatened. Sri Ramakrishna says, "A worldly man should hiss, but he shouldn't pour out his venom. He mustn't actually injure others. But he should make a show of anger to protect himself from enemies. Otherwise they will injure him. But a sannyasi need not even hiss" (*Gospel*, p. 247).

Fifth, we can cancel anger's harmful effects by sitting quietly and refusing to express them. "The physical expression of an emotion deepens the emotion, while the refusal of expression diminishes the emotion" (William James). Once the symptoms of anger appear, only a strong act of will can control them: the breath through deep, rhythmic breaths, shrillness by means of whispering, clenched fists by straightening the fingers, and rigid muscles by sitting or lying down to relax them.

We can prevent the appearance of anger only by keeping the mind calm. This leads to the sixth practical suggestion, which we should sincerely try to follow: it is better to leave the place of conflict immediately before angry symptoms appear. We can remain alone in a room with the door closed and repeat our mantra or pray, "Thy will be done" (Matthew 26:42). Remembering that "discrimination is the better part of valour," will give us courage.

The fault lies in our exclusive reliance on the intellect for our development and our neglect to practise spiritual principles side-by-side with our intellectual development. Observing that the "remote results [of physical diseases are due to] mental and immoral imbalance" Dr. Alexis Carrel noted that, "such diseases are almost unknown in social groups where life is simpler and not so agitated, where anxiety is less constant."

"In like manner," he wrote, "those who keep the peace of their inner self in the midst of the tumult of the modern city are immune from nervous and organic disorders" (*Man, The Unknown*, p. 140).

What quality of thought sets some people apart as spiritually distinctive individuals and allows them to inspire others by their peaceful attitude? This philosophical question is also a very practical one. We have largely abandoned and ignored the higher values of life. We must rediscover the fundamental unity of higher values for the sake of our survival. Perceiving man's moral and spiritual decline, Dr. Carrel observed that civilization must take note of the unified harmony of three basic laws: "life tends to conserve itself, to reproduce itself and to spiritualize itself" (*Man, The Unknown*, p. 78).

The third law refers to spiritual development and takes precedence. We disobey it at our peril, because it alone brings happiness and joy to our lives. Noting the effects of the mind upon the bodily processes, Dr. Carrel says, "When our activity is set toward a precise end, our mental and organic functions become completely harmonized." He continues:

> The unification of the desires, the application of the mind to a single purpose, produce a sort of inner peace. Man integrates himself by meditation just as by action. But he should not be content with contemplating the beauty of the ocean, of the mountains, and of the clouds, the masterpieces of the artists and the poets, the majestic constructions of philosophical thought, the mathematical formulas which express natural laws. He must also be the soul which strives to attain a moral ideal, searches for light in the darkness of this world, marches forward along the mystic way, and renounces itself in order to apprehend the

invisible substratum of the universe. (*Man, the Unknown*, pp. 140-1)

We also have the shining example of individuals who sustain crippling conditions that others find unbearable. They appear oblivious to pain, depression, self-pity and anger because they are fully integrated spiritually. The unlimited power of a spiritual mind overcomes the impact of physical and mental disease.

## TRANSFORMING VALUE OF SPIRITUAL CULTURE

Body-consciousness being the source of all misery, spiritual culture demands that we cultivate Soul-consciousness. A spiritually improved mind improves character. By controlling the senses and directing our inner vital force to something higher, greater and nobler, we transform our character and improve our quality of life with the added strength of dignity. This distinguishes us from other creatures. The basic fact that we are in essence spiritually, mentally, emotionally, psychologically and physically unified beings allows us to become spiritual and establishes our good character.

Swamiji says, "The infinite oneness of the Soul is the eternal sanction of all morality, that you and I are not only brothers—every literature voicing man's struggle towards freedom has preached that for you—but that you and I are really one. This is the dictate of Indian philosophy. This oneness is the rationale of all ethics and all spirituality" (*C. W.*, III: 189). Common ethics combined with spiritual principles are the best guidelines for secular life.

We may possess high ethical standards and accomplish praiseworthy humanitarian deeds, yet remain oblivious to our spiritual nature. One spiritual truth underlies every ethical principle: all life has a divine ground. Divinely-based ethics acquire an infinite, immortal value that is imparted to human life. Swamiji says:

> Ethics always says, "Not I, but thou." Its motto is, "Not self, but non-self." The vain ideas of individualism, to which man clings when he is trying to find that Infinite Power or that Infinite Pleasure through the senses, have to be given up . . . all codes of ethics are based upon this renunciation; destruction, not construction, of the individual on the material plane. That Infinite will never find expression upon the material plane . . . the scope, the goal, the idea of all ethics is the destruction, and not the building up, of the individual. (*C. W.*, II: 62-3)

The highest Eternal Universal Law is selflessness—giving oneself to God, in thought, word and deed and seeing God everywhere in all. "Who loves all beings, without distinction, He indeed is worshipping best his God" (*C. W.*, IV: 496).

Love for God is love for Truth. That alone gives us real happiness. In every society, we find great beings who transformed their lives through their ability to control the senses and keep their mind on Truth or Divinity. Mahatma Gandhi understood the impact of truth on human happiness. His spiritual struggle to develop his character demonstrates the triumph of the human spirit. He chose the spiritual ideal of Truth as the pole star of his life. He implemented that ideal through *Satyagraha*: non-violence, non-possession, non-stealing and chastity in thought, word and deed. Spirituality made his life complete:

> The whole of my life is saturated with the religious spirit. I could not live a single second without religion. My politics and all other activities of mine, are derived from my religion. I go further to say that every activity of a

man of religion must be derived from his religion, because religion means being bound to God, that is to say, God rules your every breath. If you recognize that truth, naturally God regulates every activity of yours. . . . In my own humble opinion, we needlessly divide life in watertight compartments, religious and others; whereas if a man has true religion in him, it must show itself in the smallest details of life" (*Gandhiji's View of Life*, pp. 133-4).

Gandhiji entered the fearsome arena of world events fearlessly due to his spiritualized cultural values. Knowingly or unknowingly, he verified the truth of Sri Ramakrishna's words, "If you enter [into the activities of] the world without first cultivating love for God, you will be entangled more and more. You will be overwhelmed with its danger, its grief, its sorrows. And the more you think of worldly things, the more you will be attached to them" (*Gospel*, pp. 81-2). If we cannot wholly dedicate ourselves to spiritual life, we can still cultivate it without abandoning our rightful duties: "Perform your duties in the world and also cultivate love of God" (Ibid., p. 703).

Systematically feeding the mind with higher values develops its spiritual resources and subdues insatiable primitive urges. Drawing from our dormant spiritual energy spiritualizes all our values. According to Professor Brightman, "Spirituality is a life of harmony, unity, and integration." He writes:

No philosophy which does not satisfy his whole mind will permanently satisfy man. Since Plato first saw this principle and used it as a pulverizing weapon against sexual sin, it has been a cornerstone of any sound philosophy of life. But what is sound is not always immediately effective. A tragic feature of human life is displayed in the violence with which man opposes his own permanent good in the interest of his temporary good, or supposed good. Passion and greed are blind but intense; and they often sweep away the power of the truest and highest ideals as if they were no more than thin air. (Edgar S. Brightman, *Nature and Values* [New York, 1945], pp. 141-2)

"Our intellect has accomplished enormous things, whilst our spiritual house has collapsed" (Jung). We are tragically adrift in a wilderness of intellectual and instinctive stimulation, compulsively obsessed with the desire for pleasure and other "culture diseases." We have lost touch with the core of our being. The unconscious mind with its built-in tensions needs "peace pills" to put it to sleep.

Contemplating the ill effects of violence, war, and natural catastrophes on society and the failure of traditional psychotherapy to remove the cause of human suffering, Jung recognized that:

> Man has always stood in need of the spiritual help which each individual's own religion held out to him. The opening up of the unconscious [referring to the limitation of Freudian analysis] always means the outbreak of intense spiritual suffering; it is as when a flourishing civilization is abandoned to invading hordes of barbarians, or when fertile fields are exposed by the bursting of a dam to a raging torrent. The World War was such an irruption [sic] which showed, as nothing else could, how thin are the walls which separate a well-ordered world from lurking chaos. But it is the same with every single human being and his reasonably ordered world. His reason has done violence to natural forces which seek their revenge and only await the moment when the partition falls to overwhelm the conscious life with destruction. Man has been aware of this danger from earliest times, even in the most primitive

stages of culture . . . Man is never helped in his suffering by what he thinks for himself, but only by revelations of a wisdom greater than his own. It is this which lifts him out of his distress." (*Modern Man in Search of a Soul*, pp. 240-1)

Every time we turn our attention to material objects, we support our mental distress and depression. We seek many therapeutic remedies and various sorts of escape when the only permanent remedy is to turn our attention to spiritual life. Wholeness and dignity come from spiritual satisfaction alone. The glory of spiritual life inspires us to ignore our lower impulses and discover the source of our creativity, freedom, joy and peace.

## LOFTY VALUES ENRICH LIFE
## WITH SPIRITUAL INSIGHT

Culture is neither predominantly intellectual nor purely utilitarian. "Man has been a dazzling success in the field of intellect and 'know-how,' and a dismal failure in the things of the spirit" (Arnold Toynbee). Assimilated ideas form our character and transform our being. Spiritual knowledge encourages enduring spiritual values that motivate us to improve our character, enriching life and bringing harmony to it. Modern values on the other hand do not take our innate integrity of character into account and are commonly associated with "pay, promotion and pension." Everything has changed in the nuclear age except desire for these three, with few exceptions.

Two remarkable communities are exempt from this prevailing modern condition. They are comparatively free from chronic illness, conflict and war. They use their own healing methods, and manage their own system of education. One is a little-known group of 12,000 people living in Gualangra, an isolated mountain peak belonging to the

Central Mountain Range of the Malay Peninsula. They were first discovered more than a century ago and are there to this day (Hun-Ming Chiang and Abraham H. Maslow, *The Healthy Personality* [New York, 1977], p. 127).

The other is a community of over 80,000 Amish people living in America for four hundred years. They live simply according to their own interpretation of biblical injunctions and the message of Christ. They do not use electricity, mass media, television, computers or automobiles. Their rejection of advanced technology and America's mainstream values has not prevented them from becoming successful and productive. Convinced of the virtue of a stoic, modest, and austere life, they continue to remain peacefully content and uncorrupted. The modern plague of consumerist culture that surrounds their borders does not afflict them. Because they are free from the stress of materialistic values and the psychic disorders that arise from them, it may be helpful to ponder the benefits of their simple, spiritual lifestyle. The Amish, the Mennonites (another similarly autonomous group that also rejects military service) and aboriginal societies that are untouched by invasions and colonization have never had to face the modern problems of stress due to their more rustic, sturdy and relatively unaffected way of life.

Community life everywhere depends on the moral and spiritual insights gained through "right conduct" applied with practicality and enthusiasm. It is time to use them. Fundamental spiritual values keep society together, harmonize the practical and the spiritual aspects of life, and nurture the virtues of renunciation and service. These values make us humane, cultured and unselfish. If we refuse to be deluded and confused by materialism and consumerism, we can enjoy the blessings of spiritual life. This is our supreme significance as humans. We must renounce the former, ineffective self-centred attitudes, and incorporate a new vision of human progress based on spiritual growth. Bertrand Russell made this appeal years ago:

> We are in the middle of a race between human skill as to means and human folly as to ends. Given sufficient folly as to ends, every increase in the skill required to achieve them is to the bad. The human race has survived hitherto owing to ignorance and incompetence; but, given knowledge and competence combined with folly, there can be no certainty of survival. Knowledge is power, but it is power for evil just as much as for good. It follows that, unless men increase in wisdom as much as in knowledge, increase of knowledge will be increase of sorrow. (Bertrand Russell, *The Impact of Science on Society*, p. 239)

No science of life that promotes the economy and well-being of individuals and society can ignore higher values. "An acquisitive society with competition as the basis and force as the arbiter in laws of conflict, where thought is superficial, people are sentimental, and morals loose, represents a civilization of power (*rajas*) and not of spirit (*sattva*) and so cannot endure" (S. Radhakrishnan).

Values are rooted in the One Supreme Reality. Somehow, we must seek that Reality and discover the Atman within. We can do this through the essential principles of Yoga: self-control, concentration, and a definite spiritual goal in life. Swamiji says, "We have to get the power to become moral; until we do that, we cannot control our actions. Yoga alone enables us to carry into practice the teachings of morality. To become moral is the object of Yoga" (*C. W.*, VIII: 43). One of the highest indispensable values we can cultivate is remembering the lives of departed saints and sages and serving the holy men and women in our midst.

## REMEMBRANCE AND FAITH IN THE HOLY ONES

Integrating our thoughts, emotions and actions strengthens and unifies our concentration. Cultivating spiritual goals may lead us to the presence of a holy person who nurtures our spirit, guides us beyond our crude conceptions of religion and increases our resolute faith in God and His grace. There are many examples of the redeeming rewards of unselfish service to others by great souls of pure character. Ida Ansell's testimony of Swami Vivekananda's extraordinary beneficence in the life of one of his devotees is an illustration. Having received loving personal guidance from Swamiji when she was sick, Edith Allan served him on occasion. At their last meeting, Swamiji told her, "If ever you are in trouble, you can call on me. No matter where I am, I'll hear you." This greatly increased Edith's faith:

> Never since the day Swamiji perceived Edith's need for help has he been out of her mind. Many times in the last fifty years she has remembered the words spoken at their last meeting... Many ordeals she has met bravely, sustained by that promise. (*Reminiscences of Swami Vivekananda by His Eastern and Western Admirers* [Calcutta, 1964], p. 392)

Mrs. Carrie Mead Wyckoff, who later donated her home for the headquarters of the Vedanta Society of Southern California, also had faith in Swamiji during times of distress. Mrs. Wyckoff's affectionate remembrance of Swamiji transformed her suffering to well-being:

> She had been suffering from some nervous ailment and had been having personal difficulties in her life. For some days the pain of her illness had been almost unbearable, and this, added to her other troubles made her feel extremely depressed. She went to the mantelpiece and

picked up Swamiji's pipe. No sooner did she have it in her hand than she heard his voice saying, "Is it so hard, Madame?" For some reason she rubbed the pipe across her forehead, and instantly the suffering left her and a feeling of well-being came over her. (Marie Louise Burke, *Swami Vivekananda: New Discoveries*, Vol. 5, p. 259)

"Be ye transformed by the renewing of your mind" (Romans, 12:2). An event in the life of Madame Calvé beautifully illustrates the words of Paul the Apostle. The celebrated vocalist was led mysteriously to Swami Vivekananda in 1894, during a tragic episode in her life. She had given the most glorious performance of her career that year at Chicago, despite a fearful premonition that had overwhelmed her, gave her stage fright, and plagued her entire performance with terrible nervousness. Returning to her room backstage after the performance, she was informed that her only child and beloved daughter had died in a fire. Her mother's anguish made her suicidal. Three times, she approached a nearby lake to drown herself. Each time, something inexplicable drew her away from it and she found herself walking on the street that led to the place where Swamiji, who was also in Chicago, was staying at that time. Though friends had told her of his redeeming spiritual power, slight doubt held her back and she did not approach him. But on her fourth or fifth attempt, she went straight to Swamiji's place in a daze, entered and sat down in a chair. Still in a daze, she heard Swamiji's voice say to her from the adjoining room, "Come, my child, don't be afraid."

She later related Swamiji's words to her: "You must forget. Become gay and happy again. Build up your health. Do not dwell in silence upon your sorrows. Transmute your emotions into some form of external expression. Your spiritual health requires it. Your art demands it." His calm, strong presence and caring suggestions left a deep impression on her mind and purified her emotions. She wrote, "It was the strength of his character, the purity and intensity of his purpose that carried conviction." Positive thoughts have spiritual power and lead us to a more satisfactory way of life. What is more, Madame Calvé's unique experience demonstrates the truth of Swamiji's assertion that "Religion can be given and taken more tangibly, more really, than anything else in the world."

The natural, genuine and unquestioning faith of these three women led them to call on Swamiji for help. Their pure faith and Swamiji's own tremendous faith in his spiritual power enabled them to receive assistance from the divine Source within him. Swamiji's purity of character wrought the wondrous release from their suffering. "As ye believe, so will it be," said Jesus. Had they been faithless and steeped in doubt, they would neither have believed in their access to Divinity nor been healed.

Hindu philosophy declares, "Do not think that you are separate from anything. Whatever you think you are separate from will circumscribe you and bind you. Think that you are one with all and you will be free." The *Brihadaranyaka Upanishad* (II. 4. 6) gives a long list of beings who ignore one who believes himself to be different from the Self in that being: "The Brahmana ignores one who knows him as different from the Self . . . The beings ignore one who knows them as different from the Self. All ignores one who knows it as different from the Self." If we are unable to see the Self in all, we feel separate, small and limited. This is the meaning.

Two additional anecdotes beautifully illustrate Swami Vivekananda's unwavering conviction of the Self and his power to bring that awareness to others. Once, when Swamiji was in Calcutta after his return from the West in 1897, he received

9

the following message from a friend: "I have got a particular disease. I am just wearing out. I am all the time in bed and cannot get up. Would you kindly come and see me? Not because I want any cure, but because I have known you, and I have heard you returned from the West and I should be very glad to see you." Swamiji immediately responded that he would. Entering the sick man's room, he simply began reciting a verse from the *Brihadaranyaka Upanishad* (II. 4. 6). His recitation alone brought new energy into the body and mind of the man, who sat up in his bed and said, "Swamiji, I feel stronger than ever." (Quoted from Swami Ashokananda, *My Philosophy and My Religion* [San Francisco, 1970], pp. 74-5). This man was actually cured and transformed. His faith in Swamiji, and Swamiji's soul-power that penetrated the heart of the man, together made his friend well.

Another time around the turn of the twentieth century, Swamiji was in San Francisco. A very ill and mentally disturbed young woman from Alameda had gone to his lecture for the first time and was very attracted to him. After attending a second lecture, she approached him with a great deal of doubt. Beckoning her to come closer, Swamiji said, "Madam, if you would like to see me privately, come to the flat tomorrow morning." This woman confided to her friends that she spent the entire night thinking of questions she would ask Swamiji. However, when she went the following morning to see him, he entered the room she was in, chanting softly and sat facing her from across the room. She related:

> All he said was, "Well, Madam." I could not speak but began to weep as though the floodgates had been opened. The Swami continued chanting for a while, then said, "Come tomorrow about the same time." All my questions were gone. All my troubles had vanished away. (Quoted

from Swami Ashokananda, *Swami Vivekananda in San Francisco* [San Francisco, 1969], pp. 26-7)

Thereafter, she attended his classes every day and received his infinite grace. He even let her cook for him. Her ability to overcome her doubt and approach Swamiji indicates her faith. "Thy faith hath made thee whole" (Matthew 10: 22). We should not let doubt and despair create a cloud over God's infinite compassion and mercy. We are all creatures of faith at the core. Whatever we place our faith in helps to form our human and spiritual character. We should trust in God and in the pure character of His saints and sages. This leads us to loftier ideals and increases our faith in the all-pervading Divinity of life.

In the *Padma Purana* and many other scriptures, we find that Indian philosophy initially regards suffering with pessimism. These scriptures transform pessimism into perfect optimism and determined faith in the Absolute that is untouched by misery and sorrow. Western as well as Eastern philosophers have made that observation:

> If Indian philosophy points relentlessly to the miseries that we suffer through shortsightedness, it also discovers a message of hope. The essence of Buddha's enlightenment— the four noble truths—sums up and voices the real view of every Indian school in this respect, namely: There *is* suffering.—There is a *cause* of suffering.—There is *cessation* of suffering.—There is a *way* to attain it. Pessimism in the Indian systems is only initial and not final. The influence of such pessimism on life is more wholesome than that of uncritical optimism. An eminent American teacher rightly points out: "Optimism seems to be more immoral than Pessimism, for Pessimism warns us of danger, while Optimism lulls us into false security" (George Herbert Palmer, *Contemporary American Philosophy*, Vol. I, p. 51).

Again, the faith in "an eternal and moral order" dominates the entire history of Indian philosophy, barring the solitary exception of the Charvaka materialists. It is the common atmosphere of faith in which all these systems, Vedic and non-Vedic, theistic and atheistic, move and breathe. (Satischandra Chatterjee and Dhirendramohan Datta, *An Introduction to Indian Philosophy* [Calcutta, 1954], pp. 14-15)

In the Pali, Latin and Hebrew languages, the word "faith" is a verb, indicating its dynamic, active quality. It is more than something we possess; it is something we do. Faith mitigates suffering and moves mountains. Numberless miracles are attributed to faith. Dependence on God unites us with the essential power of the universe. The *Bhagavad Gita* (VII: 14) says, "Verily, this *Maya* of mine, constituted of the *gunas*, is difficult to cross over; those who devote themselves to Me alone, cross over this illusion."

In the end, our faith enables us to surrender completely to His will. Sri Ramakrishna says, "He who can resign himself to the will of the Lord with simple faith and guileless devotion, attains unto Him without delay. He who has faith has all and he who lacks faith lacks all." Faith is a wonderful gift from God in which He guides us directly to Him.

# 3

# THE GREATEST MEDICAL PROBLEM OF THE CENTURY

## THE CONSCIOUS MIND AND STRESS

*The mind uncontrolled and unguided will drag us down, down, for ever—rend us, kill us; and the mind controlled and guided will save us, free us. So it must be controlled, and psychology teaches us how to do it.*

—Swami Vivekananda,
*Complete Works*, VI: 30

An immature mind enmeshed in worldly, unspiritual thoughts is the source of tension, anxiety and stress. A conscious mind nurtured by spiritual thoughts, however, can solve all stress-related problems, including those that rise from the unconscious. Knowing this, we should not allow the rich soil of the mind to lie fallow. Its proper cultivation yields the treasured crop of spiritual thoughts, purity and peace. Therefore, it is important to develop God-consciousness. "Blessed is he who carries within himself God, an ideal beauty, for therein lie springs of great thought and great action" (Louis Pasteur). In *The New Art of Science and Medicine*, a current medical journal, the *Reader's Digest* quoted a remarkably similar comment: "The only way of tackling human diseases is by purifying the soul and changing its vitiated life-stream" (Dr. Shiphard).

Man's belief that materialism, consumerism and ambition are desirable goals of life is the result of wrong tendencies rooted in immature minds. These are unspiritual goals that cause stress and illness. James Allen calls them "unlawful":

> The body is the servant of the mind. It obeys the operations of the mind, whether they be deliberately chosen or automatically expressed. At the bidding of unlawful thoughts the body sinks rapidly into disease and decay; at the command of glad and beautiful thoughts it becomes clothed with youthfulness and beauty.
>
> Disease and health, like circumstances, are rooted in thought. Sickly thoughts will express themselves through a sickly body. Thoughts of fear have been known to kill a man as speedily as a bullet, and they are continually killing thousands of people just as surely though less rapidly. The people who live in fear of disease are the people who get it. Anxiety quickly demoralizes the whole body, and lays it open to the entrance of disease; while impure thoughts, even if not physically indulged, will soon shatter the nervous system.
>
> Strong, pure and happy thoughts build up the body in vigor and grace. The body is a delicate and plastic instrument, which responds readily to the thoughts by which it is impressed, and habits of thought will produce their own effects, good or bad, upon it. (James Allen, *As a Man Thinketh* [Bombay, n.d.], pp. 21-2)

Man's interest in power, lust and greed fosters egoism, unspiritual imaginary ideas and desires, competitiveness and restlessness. Restlessness in particular is a disease that affects others. With no inclination to think deeply and no interest in contemplation or any other spiritual activity, we have nothing to offer others or ourselves. Like a strong current relentlessly pushing an uprooted tree before it until it submerges or lands in a muddy bank, these negative desires drive us inevitably to the existential abyss called "the meaninglessness of life."

Meaninglessness leads to boredom and emptiness. Schopenhauer says, "All men who are secure from want and care, now that at last they have thrown off all other burdens, become a burden to themselves. As want is the constant scourge of the people, so ennui is that of the fashionable world" (Schopenhauer, *The World as Will and Idea*, p. 404).

## ON LONELINESS

Loneliness is a breakdown of communication when the demand for attention remains unfulfilled. Constantly brooding and dwelling on loneliness makes it persist for long periods, even years and decades. One is lonely only when one thinks that this is true. With a changed attitude, the condition also changes. We are never alone. "The Kingdom of God is within you," God is the Great Indweller of all beings.

Many types of perceived loneliness have ever plagued humanity, from subtle forms to the most intense, each with its own cause. (1) *"Loneliness of vanity and narcissism"* is "the compulsive need to be praised, to be liked: for this people give up their courage [which] arises from one's sense of dignity and self-esteem" (Rollo May, *Man's Search for Himself* [New York, 1953], p. 200); (2) *"Loneliness of the outsider"* who feels generally left out and unable to participate in the game of life; (3) *"Loneliness in relationship,"* which comes from our unfulfilled desire for a compatible companion; (4) *"Loneliness of the ego"* is felt when our egoism and lack of sincerity deprive us of a loving attitude and destroy otherwise healthy relationships; (5) *"Loneliness of nostalgia"* comes from remembering past relationships and events that were perceived as pleasant, or from feeling homesick in an unfamiliar environment; (6) *"Loneliness of faith"* is keenly felt when we do not know the goal of life and lack strong faith in high ideals; (7) *"Loneliness of fantasy"* arises when our imagination fuels desire for unattainable, improbable ideals; (8) *"Loneliness of emptiness"* assails us when, after working hard all week long, we are overwhelmed by the spiritual horror of existential meaninglessness when we find time for leisure and relaxation, usually on Sundays (Viktor Frankl called this "Sunday neurosis"—some people take alcohol to diffuse their boredom. Schopenhauer puts it another way, "In the middle class, life is represented by the Sunday, and want by the six weekdays" [*The World as Will and Idea*, p. 404]); and (9) *"Loneliness of the spirit"* is "the dark night" of the soul that longs for God or the Supreme Reality, as in the case of Tolstoy.

To give life meaning, we must constantly nurture our mind with spiritual ideas and thoughts. Vedanta suggests meditation but some people think it is only for "holy people" who are willing to make a significant personal sacrifice. It is a sad mistake to feel that meditation is beyond one's capacity. In Vedanta, there is a way of meditation for everyone, according to one's individual taste and capacity.

The mind affects our mental and physical state of health or disease. In a conference organized in 1979 by the American Association for the Advancement of Science, the symposium, "The Role of Consciousness in the Physical World," took place. Several scientists represented by Dr. Willis Harman of the Stanford Research Institute (SRI) presented an innovative view at that time, which SRI supported: There is a basic interaction between mind and matter in conscious human mental activity based on the premise that mind is a valid element in the development of health and disease.

This vital, new perspective challenged the prevailing western view of reductionism, which maintains that consciousness is the result of physiological events in the body. The scientists defined four scientifically observable attributes of human consciousness: (1) mind is spatially extended; (2) mind is temporally extended; (3) mind is ultimately predominant over the physical; and (4) minds are joined [to other minds] (*Space, Time and Medicine*, p. 209). Swamiji's views on the dynamic interaction of minds to afflict or benefit humanity were mentioned in the first chapter. Swamiji further says:

> Part of our energy is used up in the preservation of our own bodies. Beyond that, every particle of our energy is day and night being used in influencing others. Our bodies, our virtues, our intellect, and our spirituality, all these are continuously influencing others; and so, conversely, we are being influenced by them. This is going on all around us. (*C. W.*, II: 13)

One's mental affliction or weakness afflicts others. We do not cultivate our mental strength. We are not sincerely interested or even genuinely curious about definite spiritual values. We are vulnerable, indiscriminate and impulsive creatures of caprice. Tragically, we waste our mental energy in many ways. Our haphazard reading habits have no definite purpose. Our garrulous arguments are selfish and satisfy only our ego. We pry into the affairs of others with misplaced uninspired curiosity. We brood, we find fault, we feel superior, we demand perfection and we impose our views on others. Ambition and egoism feed our fault-finding and brooding nature, sense of superiority and demand for perfection in others and make us impose our views on others. We gravely deplete our mental energy and purity through lust, greed, hatred, anger and jealousy. We lose precious time, energy and sleep when we disturb the mind with emotional day-dreams and fantasies. A weak mind is an unhealthy mind. It will never find peace. A strong mind is identical to a peaceful mind. Without a healthy imagination and spiritual determination in life, these wrong movements and emotions in the mind equate to mental garbage heaped up in our most precious resource.

Healthy imagination plays a key role in curing disease as well as in advancing our spiritual life. We should strive to visualize excellence in our physical well-being, since the body is the vehicle for Self-realization. Swamiji says, "When the imagination is very powerful, the object becomes visualised. Therefore by it we can bring our bodies to any state of health or disease" (*C. W.*, VI: 133). We must vigorously avow the spiritual life.

## HEALTH AND SPIRITUAL LIFE : THE TERRIBLE COST OF DISAVOWAL

The ancient enduring science of Ayurveda defines health as *svasthya*, "to be one's own spiritual self." In this state, the three Ayurvedic principles of air (*vata*), bile (*pitta*) and phlegm (*kapha*) are in balance with the contented senses, mind and soul. "The doctor who does not find out the inner state of the mind of the patient by the light of his knowledge cannot find out the disease" is a key precept of Ayurveda. One of its fundamental principles is holistic treatment or the care of the unified body, mind and soul. Its definition of functional health is straightforward: "To be healthy is to have the ability, despite an occasional bout of illness, to live with full use of your faculties and to be vigorous, alert and happy to be alive, even in old age." Living according to spiritual principles brings forth great energy from our inner resources. We can use it for a vigorous, purposeful lifestyle with a determined will to make the most of our potential.

Swamiji says, "We must learn that nothing can happen to us, unless we make ourselves susceptible to it. I have just said, no disease can come to me until the body is ready; it does not depend alone on the germs, but upon a certain predisposition which is already in the body" (C. W. II: 7). Swamiji would assert his soul-force to remove his fatigue whenever he felt weak and exhausted. He embodied fearlessness. From his store of practical experiences, Swamiji once told his disciples:

> The other day, I was a guest of Babu Priyanath Mukherjee at Baidyanath. There I had such a spell of asthma that I felt like dying. But from within, with every breath arose the deep-toned sound, "I am He, I am He." Resting on the pillow, I was waiting for the vital breath to depart, and observing all the time that from within was being heard the sound of, "I am He, I am He!" I could hear all along ... — The Brahman, the One without a second, alone exists, nothing manifold exists in the world. (C. W., VII: 137)

Disavowal of our true nature makes us weak. Weakness is removed by the strength of positive spiritual avowal. Swamiji says:

> Do not talk of the wickedness of the world and all its sins. . . . The world is made weaker and weaker every day by such teachings. Men are taught from childhood that they are weak and sinners. Teach them that they are all glorious children of immortality, even those who are the weakest in manifestation. Let positive, strong, helpful thought enter into their brains from very childhood. Lay yourselves open to these thoughts, and not to weakening and paralysing ones. . . . That is the Truth; The infinite

strength of the world is yours. Drive out the superstition that has covered your minds. Let us be brave. Know the Truth and practise the Truth. The goal may be distant, but awake, arise, and stop not till the goal is reached. (*C. W.*, II: 87)

We may feel isolated, betrayed and less healthy if we lack inner spiritual conviction. Author Norman Cousins calls this confidence the "belief system." It is so significant that he dedicated the last chapter of *Human Options* to his observations regarding the impact of the human belief system on the healing system of the body. He writes:

The two work together. The healing system is the way the body mobilizes all its resources to combat disease. The belief system is often the activator of the healing system. The belief system represents the unique element in human beings that makes it possible for the human mind to affect the workings of the body. How one responds— intellectually, emotionally or spiritually—to one's problems has a great deal to do with the way the human body functions. One's confidence, or lack of it, in the prospects of recovery from serious illness affects the chemistry of the body. The belief system converts hope, robust expectations, and the will to live into plus factors in any contest of forces involving disease. The belief system is no substitute for competent medical attention in serious illness or vice versa. Both are essential. The belief system is not just a state of mind. It is a prime physiological reality . . . The greatest force in the human body is the natural drive of the body to heal itself—but that force is not independent of the belief system, which can translate expectations into physiological change. Nothing is more wondrous about the fifteen billion neurons in the human brain than their ability to convert thoughts, hopes, ideas, and attitudes into chemical substances. Everything begins, therefore, with belief. What we believe is the most powerful option of all. (Norman Cousins, *Human Options*, p. 205)

Sociologist Ernest R. Mowrer (b. 1895) writes, "Many sources of present evidence indicate that most—perhaps all— neurotic human beings suffer, not because they are unduly inhibited as regards their biological drives, but because they have disavowed and repudiated their own moral strivings. Anxiety, I believe, comes, not from repressed sexuality or pent-up hatred, but from a denial and defiance of the forces of conscience." Carl Jung writes:

> The moral attitude is a real factor in life with which the psychologist must reckon if he is not to commit the gravest errors. The psychologist must also remember that certain religious convictions not founded on reason are a necessity of life for many persons. It is again a matter of psychic realities which can cause and cure diseases. How often have I heard a patient exclaim, "If only I knew that my life had some meaning and purpose, then there would be no silly story about my nerves!" (*Modern Man in Search of a Soul*, pp. 193-4)

Spiritual thoughts and actions uphold our conscience. Writes Jung, "The psychotherapist must even be able to admit that the ego is ill for the very reason that it is cut off from the whole and has lost its connection with mankind as well as with the spirit" (Ibid., p. 123). We will always need the spiritual help and essential strength of our religion. After noting that "Freud has unfortunately overlooked the fact that man has never yet been able single-handedly to hold his own against the powers of darkness" (Ibid., p. 240), Jung declared, "Man is never helped in his suffering by what he thinks for himself, but only by revelations of a wisdom greater than his own. It is this that lifts him out of his darkness" (Ibid., p. 241).

The "real pathology of our age" is that in spite of the fact that stress underlines the need for healthy spiritual values in life, we outright reject, conceal or repress our religious feeling. We refuse to let spiritual values permanently shape our mind to provide the sense of security and protection we crave.

We can begin by discriminating between what is real and unreal. Plato used the terms "Good" and "Evil." He wrote, "No attempt should be made to cure the body without treating the Soul." He emphasized the importance of this kind of knowledge:

> It is not the life of knowledge, not even if it includes all the sciences, that creates happiness and well-being, but a single branch of knowledge—the science of Good and Evil. If you exclude this from other branches, medicine will be equally able to give us health; shoe-making, shoes; weaving, cloths; steamships will still save life at sea and strategy win battles. But without knowledge of Good and Evil, the use and the excellence of these sciences will be found to have failed us. (Plato, *Charmides*, p. 74)

According to Plato, three elements—a monster, a lion and a man—assume a dual partnership of lower and higher consciousness in making us fully human. The monster represents primitive physical urges and the lion represents ambition; these two elements signify our lower consciousness. The third element, man, is the spiritual aspect of Plato's idea and represents our higher consciousness. Knowledge of all three provides balance in life. He wrote, "The greatest mistake physicians can make is that they attempt to cure the body without attempting to cure the mind; yet the mind and body are one and should not be treated separately!"

Plato looked to politics and ethics to support his idea of the integrated personality. Vedanta on the other hand, describes the integrated personality as one who has an awareness of the timeless, eternal and infinite Truth, which is expressed as life due to the hidden influence of the Supreme Reality behind it. Without this awareness, we cannot have an integrated personality. Our lack of spiritual awareness and consequent ignorance of the Self makes us vulnerable to stress, suffering and sorrow.

## STRESS IMPLICATES PSYCHOSOMATIC ILLNESS

Our greatest medical problem, stress, is the least understood. The stress concept originated with Canadian endocrinologist Hans Selye, who defined it as the "rate of wear and tear in the human body." He identified mental stress ("stressor") as the root cause of common modern illnesses (hypertension, peptic ulcers, etc.). Mental stress stimulates the hypothalamus, which controls the autonomic nervous system in the brain. The hypothalamus in turn activates the pituitary gland, which secretes ACTH, the stress hormone. ACTH then stimulates the secretion of other hormones and steroids such as adrenalin. During stress, the adrenal cortex reacts by releasing a large quantity of a steroidal hormone called cortisol. Increased blood sugar levels, high blood pressure and other significant changes in the body activate varying levels of stress beyond our normal tolerance level, i.e., stress that causes illness which endangers the entire organism. These are some of the serious physical effects when we live in constant stress.

In his Preface to *The Stress of Life*, Selye wrote:

> . . . although we cannot avoid stress as long as we live, we
> can learn a great deal about how to keep its damaging

side effects to a minimum . . . many common diseases are largely due to errors in our adaptive response to stress, rather than to direct damage by germs, poisons, or other external agents. In this sense many nervous and emotional disturbances, high blood pressure, cardiovascular, and renal diseases appear to be essentially *diseases of adaptation.* (Hans Selye, *The Stress of Life* (New York / Toronto / London, 1956), p. viii)

Selye concluded that stress has significant psychosomatic implications and long-term psychological consequences throughout our lives. He advises, "Fight always for the highest attainable aim, but never put up resistance in vain" (*The Stress of Life*, p. 253).

Fear occasionally cloaks itself in the garment of physical pain, we all know. An entire range of psychosomatic illnesses, from the common cold to paralyzing arthritis, often originates from "deep-seated fears and a sense of guilt." A scar on the body is less disturbing than the scar in one's character. Jung's claim that his thousands of patients over age thirty-five "all have been people whose problem in the last resort was that of finding a religious outlook on life" is often quoted legitimately. Every neurosis indicates a lack of intellectual and emotional satisfaction in a spiritual outlook on life. "What we are, that we behold, and what we behold, that we are." Neurosis stems from egoism, guilt, fear and hatred. In his book, *Man Against Himself,* Karl Menninger discusses what he perceives as the cause of neurosis: living with the wrong attitude. Neurotics invite their own troubles and refuse to outgrow them. Afraid of examining their troubles from a correct perspective, they ruin themselves by clinging to their depressed moods. In *The Magic Mountain*, Thomas Mann brilliantly portrays the sad portrait of human negativity. It may just be simpler to be ill than to face the challenges of life. A self-centred, self-pitying, immature life is the subject of poet laureate John Masefield's illuminating poem, *The Harm I Have Done in Being Me*. The modern agnostic is a tragic figure with a shattered frame of mind.

Emotional insecurity leads to the major symptoms of worry, self-pity, anger and depression. The leading role of emotions in our mental and physical state has been widely observed by doctors:

> We are all familiar with the term "emotionally induced illness." Doctors today indicate that seventy to eighty-five percent of all physical ailments are provoked by emotional disturbance. Such debilitating diseases as heart trouble, high blood pressure, ulcers, asthma, and some forms of arthritis derive from emotional tension. Dr. S. I. McMillan in his excellent book, *None of These Diseases*, states that there are fifty-one emotionally induced diseases. That is why a depressed person feels sickly if he indulges his depression for a protracted period.
>
> Emotions are not generated spontaneously. Our emotions flow from the thinking pattern of the mind. Suppose, for example, that you are spontaneously asked to come to the platform and address a large audience. If you are not trained for that kind of experience, your mind will immediately set up self-conscious thought patterns producing fear or fright, which in turn will effect a physiological change in your body. Your uneasiness will occasion knocking knees and restricted saliva glands. Your normal voice may be completely restricted, creating a high or screechy sound. Thus emotional tension, fashioning a rapid chain reaction, affects the entire body. (*How to Win Over Depression*, p. 64)

Neurobiologists and other medical researchers confirm the complex interdependence between the mind and body during states of health and illness. Psychoneuroimmunology, a new science that studies the interactions of the mind, the brain, and the body, promises to enhance the practical applications of their finding. Researchers at the National Institute of Mental Health at Bethesda, Maryland have given convincing evidence that depressed mental states as well as high or low blood pressure, sleeplessness, and asthma are brought on by fear and anxiety. They affect the body's immune system, which protects us against viruses, infections, and non-infectious diseases like cancer.

The *British Medical Journal* and other prestigious medical journals recently reported that simple *Pranayama* techniques calm the restless mind in the treatment of asthma. This suggests its usefulness in healing psychosomatic illnesses. *Pranayama* can be practised only by people leading a moderate, ethical and quiet life. Swami Vivekananda says, "There must be perfect chastity in thought, word and deed; without it the practice of Raja-Yoga is dangerous, and may lead to insanity. If people practise Raja-Yoga and at the same time lead an impure life, how can they expect to become Yogis?" (*C. W.*, I: 170).

*Pranayama* must be learned from a qualified teacher. Swamiji says:

> The first lesson is just to breathe in a measured way, in and out. That will harmonise the system. When you have practised this for some time, you will do well to join to it the repetition of some word as "Om," or any other sacred word. . . .

> The easiest way is to stop the right nostril with the thumb, and then slowly draw in the breath through the left; then

close both nostrils with thumb and forefinger, and imagine that you are sending that current down . . .; then take the thumb off, and let the breath out through the right nostril. Next inhale slowly through that nostril, keeping the other closed by the forefinger, then close both, as before. The way the Hindus practise this would be very difficult for this country, because they do it from their childhood, and their lungs are prepared for it. Here it is well to begin with four seconds, and slowly increase. Draw in four seconds, hold in sixteen seconds, then throw out in eight seconds. This makes one *Pranayama*. (*C. W.*, I: 166-8 passim)

The principle of *Pranayama* requires a spiritual attitude and pure thoughts. When inhaling, one should concentrate the mind on aspects of purity and holiness. When exhaling, one should release all negative thoughts and impressions from the mind:

*Pranayama* should be practised with closed eyes. Instead of meditating then on the form of the Chosen Ideal, direct your attention to the breathing exercises, keeping the required numbers by the *Japa* of your Mantra, counting on the fingers of the left hand, in the usual way. These processes should be learnt from the Guru. While inhaling, think that you are drawing within yourself purity, compassion, strength, courage and other godly virtues; and while exhaling, think that you are ejecting from within all imperfections, such as evil thoughts, impurity, narrowness, envy and sinful tendencies. (Swami Virajananda, *Towards the Goal Supreme, Paramartha Prasanga*, [Kolkata, 2004], pp. 30-1)

*Pranayama* practised correctly and with a pure motive rouses the coiled up energy at the base of the spine known as

*Kundalini.* Swami Vivekananda says, "The rousing may come in various ways, through love for God, through the mercy of perfected sages, or through the power of the analytic will of the philosopher" (*C. W.*, I: 165). *Pranayama* more effectively removes impurities and stress from the mind than do the temporary means of other, external treatments such as psychotropic medicines and the like.

Psychosomatic illnesses appear after we have been harbouring lower impulses in the mind for a long time. This is no light matter today. Children as young as five are receiving psychotropic medicines to control deviant behaviours. Like their elders, they are attending yoga classes or receiving music therapy to relieve them of mental and emotional stress in addition to managing the pain of physical illness. Music therapy, as a supplement to medicine, has gained legitimacy in recent years in the United States and other western countries where it is widely practised in schools for children with special needs, in hospitals and in mental institutions to manage pain, reduce emotional stress and mitigate serious mental complexes associated with physical and mental disabilities. The remedy of music is also an additional therapy to medical treatment in the East, in China, Japan, and India, where the *raga*, the "miracle of microtones," indicates great potential for research into its power to encourage therapeutic benefits, including improved motor coordination and socialization. The physical, emotional and mental stress of children should give us cause for a greater concern to improve our way of life. One doctor has said:

Seventy percent of all patients who come to physicians could cure themselves if they only got rid of their fears and worries. Don't think for a moment that I mean their ills are imaginary. Their ills are as real as a throbbing toothache and sometimes a hundred times more serious. I refer to such illnesses as nervous indigestion, some stomach ulcers, heart disturbances, insomnia, some headaches, and some types of paralysis.

Fear causes worry. Worry makes you tense and nervous and affects the nerves of your stomach and actually changes the gastric juices of your stomach from normal to abnormal and often leads to stomach ulcers. (*How to Stop Worrying and Start Living*, p. 25)

Psychosomatic illness actually reflects the insecurity, tension, confusion, and overwhelming complexity of modern living. In addition to long-term worries and fears, contemporary life engenders "supreme selfishness" and the inability to adapt to reality. Every day, newspapers record the tragic consequences of stress among ambitious or highly pressured executives and business people. When their efforts do not satisfy their greed, they are worn down with frustration, anxiety, fear, defeat and despair. They sometimes die young. Many turn to various forms of exercise for relief but there is observable evidence that physical exercise can be harmful unless it is accompanied by a relaxed, peaceful, and therefore, happy mind. Fritjof Capra observes the ultimate effects of good or ill health:

Health is really a multidimensional phenomenon involving interdependent physical, psychological and social aspects. The common representation of health and illness as opposite ends of one dimensional continuum is quite misleading. Physical disease may be balanced by a positive mental attitude and social support, so that the overall state is one of well-being. On the other hand, emotional problems or social isolation can make a person feel sick in spite of physical fitness. . . . What is unhealthy for the individual is generally also unhealthy for the society and for the embedding ecosystem. (Fritjof Capra, *The Turning Point* [London, 1982], pp. 355-54).

Decades ago, a psychologist claimed that infants are more readily infected with the fear and loathing of other people around them than they are by infectious diseases. "But fortunately," he observed, "infants can also catch love and goodness and faith and so grow up to become normal, healthy children and adults" (*The Power of Positive Thinking*, pp. 212-13). This is not a simplistic view. Physicians have long observed that people with unconscious, long-term grudges, resentments or hate against someone often suffer joint and muscle disease, skin rashes, allergies, ulcers, high blood sugar, etc. Our inner chronic maladies make their appearance in external chronic conditions.

## PERSONAL REVERSALS
## THROUGH SPIRITUAL VALUES

In *Mind and Body—Psychosomatic Medicine*, psychiatrist Helen Flanders Dunbar, M. D. related the case of a diabetic woman seeking her help. Although the patient was happily married with children and appeared content with her life, diabetic neuritis had set in with no medical cause. In therapy, the patient discovered she had a deep-seated resentment and hatred towards her tyrannical mother. She learned that "annoyance, rage, and fear caused more sugar in her blood than potatoes, candy and ice-cream" (*Mind and Body* [New York, 1947], pp. 61-2. Quoted from *Adventures in Vedanta*, p. 65). When she let these feelings go, the pain and stiffness left her.

Stomach ulcers manifest directly from specific bacterial infections, but they also have an emotional component. Another patient in psychotherapy observed that his stomach ulcer acted up whenever he was near his aggressive wife. The ulcer did not bother him when he went away on business trips. He learned that trying to change her behaviour was futile but he could change his own. He altered his outlook towards his wife (who loved him in spite of her aggression) and the ulcer disappeared (Ibid.).

The more serious case of a woman who developed fatal hydrophobia after a rabid dog bit her is a cautionary tale. Her doctor suggested she write her last will and testament before she lost her mental faculties. She scribbled busily for a long time. Looking curiously at what she wrote, the doctor saw a long list of names and realized her mind was already damaged. When he asked her what it meant, she said, "I am making a list of those I'm going to bite" (Quoted from *Adventures in Vedanta*, p. 67). If we continue to cultivate the lower self by identifying with the body and mind, the unhealthy thoughts and feelings we harbour will cause us to have a similar fate on our deathbed. We cannot live our entire lives nurturing our lower impulses and expect to get rid of them when the last moment arrives.

Lucy Freeman worked as a reporter for *The New York Times*. For over two decades, she suffered from depression and was gripped by various physical illnesses. One, in particular, caused her devastating pain. Whenever she got depressed, she would catch a cold "to punish" herself. The sinusitis that always accompanied her cold was so severe and painful that it made her wish she were dead. The narrow and dogmatic views she had come to accept did not give her any assurance about the meaning and purpose of life or the means to overcome suffering. No doctor had been able to cure her. She could not understand what caused her unremitting pain because she lacked the greater insight of self-knowledge. As a last resort, she turned to a psychoanalyst for help.

Her psychoanalyst was like a spiritual advisor to her in the sense that he encouraged her to face her unconscious fear of death. When she began to understand herself better in therapy, her self-understanding and self-acceptance increased. Her tearful struggle to eradicate her fear and anger made her sinusitis gradually disappear. "My tears set free my nose," she wrote. She no longer needed medications for pain and sleep. She acquired a healthier, more relaxed lifestyle. Her popular books on the subject of fear provide firsthand reports about her condition and its cure. She writes:

> I believe everyone wants to love and be loved and that happiness stems from a facing and acceptance of self that allows you to give and receive love.

> Some think of love as a passionate, hungry, dramatic feeling, all-consuming in intensity and desire. As I see it, this is, rather, immature love; it is a demand on others, not a giving of oneself. Mature love, the love that brings happiness, flows out of an inner fullness, and accepts, understands and is tender towards the other person. It does not ask to be served but only where it may serve.

> Six years ago, I could hardly breathe because of acute sinus. My stomach was always upset and full of queasiness and I had trouble sleeping, even though I felt exhausted all the time. In desperation after doctors who treated the physical symptoms failed to ease the pain, I tried psychoanalysis. I was lucky to find a wise, compassionate man who showed me what it meant to be able to trust myself and others.

> The physical ills are gone, but more than that, I have at long last started to acquire a philosophy of living. I had never possessed one. I had lived on dogma and dicta which I had accepted unquestioningly through the years, even

though I believed little of it, because I feared to question. But by being unable to live naturally and at peace with myself I was flying in the face of nature. She was punishing me with illness, and, at the same time, informing me all was not well, just in case I wanted to do something about it.

In order to change, I needed help in facing myself. For me it was not easy to "know thyself." All my life I had accepted the lesser of the two evils and run away from self because truth was more dangerous. Once I thought that to survive, I had to put on a mask and forget what lay underneath. But masks are false protections and the inner part of me refused to go unheard forever. It caught up eventually, and unless it was to master me I had to face such feelings as fear, anger, envy, hatred, jealousy and excessive need for attention. When I realized I could not have done anything else except what I did, I was able to like myself more and be able to like others not for what they could give me but for what I could give to them.

The Bible shows the way to easy, happy living in many of its pages. It advises, "It is more blessed to give than to receive." Those who expect the most are apt to receive the least. I had expected much and was filled with fury because nothing in the outside world relieved my emptiness and despair. Nothing did, either, until I could face the anger and fury, the emptiness and despair, and slowly start to know such new feelings as compassion, conviction, control, calm. I learned, too, of reason—that judicious combination of thought and feeling that enables me to take more responsibility for myself and others, that allows me to slay the ghosts of the past.

For me there is much hard work ahead to achieve greater happiness. Yet, the very struggle I have put into achieving a measure of it makes happiness that much more dear. (Lucy Freeman, "A Mask Was Stifling Me." Quoted from *This I Believe: The Living Philosophies of One Hundred Thoughtful Men and Women in All Walks of Life*, Edward P. Morgan, ed. [New York, 1952], pp. 57-8)

Most of us try to relieve our unbearable symptoms rather than find and remove their root cause. Lucy Freeman silenced those who doubted her *overall* cure from introspective self-analysis by maintaining that her acute sinusitis was definitely gone for good—giving them the tangible result that they could understand and grasp. However, she defended the method of looking within to improve one's character and self-assurance as well as to find the cause of one's illness. In her pioneering autobiographical account of her psychoanalysis, *Fight against Fears*, a bestseller that sold over a million copies, she wrote:

Some (unanalyzed [persons] of course) charge [that] analysis kills [the] ability to feel. For me it heightened awareness of self and others, allowing me to feel with more assurance instead of groping with confusion.

I felt more comfortable with myself and, therefore with others who inherited the earth to do with as they wish. I accepted the world more as it was, merged with both its misery and merriment. Browning wrote, "When the fight begins within himself, a man's worth something." I felt the fight was being waged more within me, less with those around me.

I no longer blamed misfortune or bemoaned what happened. (Lucy Freeman, *Fight Against Fears* [New York, 1951], p. 304)

Lucy Freeman did not openly state what it was that cured her. In our estimation, the psychological balance a patient achieves through analysis comes when the "center of gravity which has been centered in others comes to rest within himself."

In still another case, a thirty-nine-year-old woman suffered various physical ailments for eighteen years after marrying a man she regarded as inferior. Traditional medicine and alternative treatments for her pains, dizziness and general weakness gave her no relief. In psychotherapy, she discovered that she harboured two deep resentments: the burdensome care of her parents and her sister's neglect of their needs. Even the birth of a child had not made her happy. Her condition persisted. Encouraged by the therapist, she began to see the connection between her psychic and physical symptoms. She realized that her own repressed anger was triggering her sickly condition. Slowly, her mind became balanced and she adopted a more accepting attitude. She was cured of her psychosomatic illness and achieved harmony in her life (*Mind and Body*, pp. 49-52. Quoted from *Adventures in Vedanta*, p. 94).

Alcoholics Anonymous (AA) is a worldwide group of over a million alcohol-addicted people. They help each other solve the problems of alcoholism and its related illnesses and stress. AA identifies human suffering as the result of the "Seven Deadly Sins" of pride, greed, lust, anger, gluttony, envy and sloth. When indulgence in our lower instincts is our sole objective in life, pride justifies our actions and cheats us of life's true significance and goal. AA members practise the "Twelve Steps". Based on the idea of unity, they are remarkably spiritual. AA's familiar prayer in all times of emotional stress and spiritual weakness is uttered in silence: "God grant me the serenity to accept the things I cannot change, courage to change the things I can, and wisdom to know the difference. Thy will, not mine, be done."

Resentments and anger lodged deep in the subconscious mind have long manifested in neurological illnesses that are still common today. More than half a century ago, *American Magazine* (October 1947) described a woman who had reached an extreme point in her life. She heard of a clinic founded on spiritual principles and went there for help:

> A thirty-four-year-old woman came to this clinic. She looked like a woman of fifty and had for months suffered from insomnia, nervousness and chronic fatigue. She had consulted doctors, but to no avail. Religious at heart, she tried to pray but without success. She finally became so depressed that she wanted to commit suicide. The clinic psychiatrist discovered the real cause of her illness: a deep resentment towards her sister who had married the man she herself wanted to marry. Outwardly, she was kind to her sister, but deep in her subconscious mind, she cherished a terrible hatred which ruined her mental and physical health. Then a minister came to her aid. "You know it is evil to hate. You must ask God to help you to forgive your sister in your heart; then God will give you peace. She followed this advice. "Through prayer and faith in a power greater than herself she has been able to forgive her sister. Her depression and insomnia are gone. She is a new person and happier than ever before." (Swami Yatiswarananda, *Adventures in Religious Life* (Chennai, 1959), pp. 159-60)

Her case highlights the virtue of forgiveness. It is a gracious, divine impulse in the human mind that stirs us to righteous action. Complete forgiveness allows us to forget and live more happily. If we have an expansive view, we are able to forgive. If we harbour a contracted view, we cannot forgive others or ourselves. The positive effects of a spiritual perspective transformed this woman's mental and emotional outlook and increased her capacity for a more spiritual way of life.

Another similar example highlights the fact that "emotions and feelings are quite as real as germs and no less respectable. The resultant pain and suffering of diseases caused primarily by the emotions are no more imaginary than those caused by bacteria" (Norman Vincent Peale). A woman affected with rheumatoid arthritis suffered from eczema on her hands. The surgeon she approached for help referred her to a psychiatrist. After a few sessions, the psychiatrist was able to penetrate her unyielding, tight-lipped attitude enough to find the underlying cause of her external symptoms. She was holding on to her perception that her younger brother had always treated her unfairly. When she resolved her feelings with her brother, she gave up her hate and resentment. The eczema disappeared in due course (*Power of Positive Thinking*, p. 214).

"One must bring philosophy to medicine and medicine to philosophy" (Hippocrates). The medical community is gradually accepting the fact that medicines represent only one element in the cure of diseases and chronic stress. Harnessing the power of thought, imagination and meditation allows us to overcome all physical and mental weakness and arrive at Truth. Swamiji says:

> There is only one power to cure the body, and that is in every man. Medicine only rouses this power. Disease is only the manifest struggle of that power to throw off the poison which has entered the body. Although the power to overthrow poison may be roused by medicine, it may be more permanently roused by the force of thought. Imagination must hold to the thought of health and strength in order that in case of illness, the memory of the

ideal of health may be roused and the particles [of the brain] re-arranged in the position into which they fell when healthy. The tendency of the body is then to follow the brain. (*C. W.*, VI: 133)

Two remarkable case studies illustrate this principle in action. They provide two important pieces of evidence: The perception of pain and lack of wellness is tied to our perception of time; health can be re-established by the power of imagination aided by visualization. A six-year-old boy, Mark, suffered from hyperactivity, the "hurry sickness". The method of biofeedback was introduced to the child when his symptoms and inability to complete normal tasks became unbearable for his parents, teachers and classmates, who were unable to help him. He readily mastered the biofeedback techniques because he made a logical connection between mentally inducing and controlling calmness in his body and manipulating the biofeedback instruments successfully to cure himself of his nervous condition and train his mind to continue to accomplish beneficial behaviours. When the biofeedback therapist asked the child, "What happened to all the nervousness inside you?" Mark answered, "It's gone now. When I feel that way I just let it go out through my big toes!" Mark had discovered that he could visualize his nervousness as a tangible substance. He could stand aside mentally, uninfluenced by time and space, and witness his own condition. In other words, he could sufficiently distance himself from it spatially and temporally. Witnessing his hyperactive tendencies, he was able to neutralize them and change his own behaviour (*Space, Time & Medicine*, p. 172).

The power of imagination and visualization that can be brought to bear in biofeedback techniques also alleviated the physical suffering of another patient. Monica was able to visualize the pain in the left side of her neck resulting from a skiing accident as a small, glowing, red ball. Concentrating mentally on it, she manipulated the ball after it became extremely vivid in her mind. She then removed it from her body to a central space six feet in front of her. It grew to the size of a basketball and hovered before her, suspended in time and space even though other events went on normally. She further manipulated this tangible visualization of her pain by using her imagination to make it change colours. When it appeared as white, it shrank to its original size, whereupon she replaced it in the left side of her neck. During such episodes, biofeedback instruments recorded Monica's very low muscle tension and she reported that her pain greatly lessened or disappeared. Within a few weeks, her pain ceased altogether (Ibid., p. 173).

## ROLE OF HOLISTIC HEALTH

The holistic health movement was a reaction to the failure of Western medicine — which emphasises the analytical and mechanical aspects of medicine, to address serious issues of unrest that caused social imbalance in the West. The American Holistic Medical Association was founded in 1978, followed by the British Holistic Medical Association a few years later. The medical research of Pavlov and K. M. Bykov demonstrated (1924) that the involuntary processes mediated by the autonomic nervous system could be brought under voluntary control by the mind. Today, holistic health practitioners have established that individual organs and entire systems of organs, i.e., the circulatory, respiratory, digestive systems, etc., can come under our control and regulation to a certain degree merely by changing our mental attitude and consequent style of life.

In addition, Sigmund Freud brought attention to the role of the unconscious in psychosomatic illness. His student Alfred Adler in turn demonstrated that unconscious behaviour could be transformed by the ego. Psychiatry and clinical psychology were added to the field of medical science. Holistic medicine now recognizes the important role of the mind in health and that social, economic, environmental and political influences affect mental and physical health. This is a brief summary of the significance of holistic health.

Holistic health does not provide the single remedy of taking a prescribed medication for a specific period in order to heal an illness. It may include medication for certain conditions but it always involves some form of sacrifice as well as patience over a long period to achieve the desired result. The purified and controlled higher mind is characterized by truth and must replace the false or impure lower self, composed of all our unrestrained instincts, drives and impulses. This aspect of the work is done through the mind. The mind is one. Though it is unified, one part of the mind, drawn by worldly attractions, remains on the lower level of existence. Another part of the mind, attracted to higher spiritual thoughts, dwells in the higher realms of being. The *Bhagavad Gita* (VI: 5-6) says,

> Raise yourself by yourself;
>     don't let yourself down,
>   for you alone are your own friend,
>       you alone are your own enemy.

> One becomes one's own friend
>     when one has conquered oneself;
>   But to the unconquered self,
>       he or she is inimical (and becomes)
>       like (an external) enemy.

Lack of harmony between the higher and lower self leads to inner conflict and confusion. We should not allow deeply ingrained harmful habits, both conscious and unconscious, such as addictions, fears, morbid thoughts of death and suicidal ideation, pleasure-gratification, etc., to dominate our life. We must give them up as part of the holistic treatment programme designed to activate the body's inherent potential for self-renewal through conscious awakening of love, friendliness and peacefulness within. When the lower self is purified through spiritual practices, harmful qualities are checked or restrained. Love for the higher self dawns when we begin to regard the human body as an instrument through which Divinity manifests. The *Maitreyi Upanishad* (2. 1) says that the body is "the temple of the indwelling Spirit." The body is the temple of God and the means by which we worship Him through service. Hindu scriptures mention five ways to serve God, through service to the gods, the sages, the manes, human beings and animals. The ancient lawgiver Manu says, "Through the repeated practice of these five great *yajnas* (sacrifices), the human body gets divinized" (*Manu-samhita* 2.28). This is the underlying philosophy of holistic health.

Most holistic health programmes today include some form of meditation. Directors of large and small corporations have also discovered that employees concentrate better and work more efficiently with a mind made more relaxed and peaceful through meditation. Many offer in-house meditation courses to their employees.

For our purposes here, holistic health may be defined as that state of equilibrium which brings man's inner vital force into harmony with the external world. Plutarch says, "Choose the best life, and custom will render it agreeable." The beneficial practice of regulating thoughts, actions, exercise, relaxation and sleep, together with opening the entire mind-body complex to the source of the divine Power within becomes an excellent, agreeable and valuable habit in the spiritual path. An integrated, holistic approach achieves harmony within and without. It removes stress and the attitudes of hopelessness, fear and rigid thinking that prevent healing. Medical research supports this point of view. Dr. Deepak Chopra writes:

> It is fascinating that a major study of four hundred spontaneous remissions of cancer, later interpreted by Elmer and Alyce Green of the Menninger Clinic, found that all the patients had only one thing in common—every person had changed his attitudes before the remission occurred, finding some way to become hopeful, courageous, and positive. In other words, they broke down their indoctrination. (Deepak Chopra, M. D., *Quantum Healing* [New York, 1990], p. 162)

## CULTURAL IMPLICATIONS OF
## MEDICAL RESEARCH

Medical research on meditation has broad cultural implications. On the one hand, medical professionals use meditation techniques to help patients inhibit, control or prevent the painful effects of chronic diseases and to restore balance when depression, attention-deficit disorder, hyperactivity, infertility, and other disturbing or life-threatening conditions like cancer and AIDS present themselves. The academic community supports this work. Over two hundred universities worldwide have provided the setting for experimental studies on meditation, including Harvard University, Harvard Medical School, Boston University, Massachusetts Institute of Technology, Princeton

University, University of Chicago, and George Washington University, among many others.

On the other hand, hospitals, schools and universities throughout the world are teaching and practising meditation. The addition of courses in holistic and alternative medicine with titles such as "Caring for the Soul" is on the rise in medical schools. According to a survey of all medical schools in the late 1990s by Dr. Wallace Sampson of Stanford University, the majority of schools presented these courses without bias. In England, students at the Manchester Business School meditate prior to their daily creative ideas session (Swami Jitatmananda, *Value Education* [Rajkot: Ramakrishna Ashrama, 2003], p. 66). Rooms marked, "Meditation," exist at airports, hotels, law firms, government buildings and within prisons.

Articles on meditation have been published in the *International Journal of Comparative and Applied Criminal Justice* as well as in other prominent journals, including *American Journal of Hypertension, American Journal of Physiology, American Journal of Psychiatry, Western Psychologist, British Journal of Educational Psychology, British Journal of Psychology, Social Indicators Research,* and *Psychologia—An International Journal of Psychology in the Orient*.

Millions of adult Americans claim to practise meditation daily. Readers may be greatly benefited if they read "Just Say Om," a lengthy article by Joel Stein published in *Time Magazine* (August 4, 2003). He provides an up-to-date review of the broad impact of meditation upon western culture and medical practice, including scientists, school and university students, judges of the Supreme Court, politicians and film stars. Stein mentions that the official number of Americans practising meditation on *Om* is ten million. In addition, it is estimated today that twenty million people, individually or in groups, are practising Yoga.

## SCIENCE AND THE BENEFITS OF MEDITATION

When the two spiritual principles of faith in a higher Being or Principle and humaneness unite with meditation, our quality of life improves tremendously. The current popular awareness of the positive effects of spiritual life that centres on the various techniques of meditation is making the scientific community gradually notice the benefits of meditation on the mind and body.

Eastern spiritual principles and Western science have come together to address the global problem of stress. Research on meditation "for 30 years . . . has told us that it works beautifully as an antidote to stress . . . What's exciting about the new research is how meditation can train the mind and reshape the brain," according to Daniel Goleman, author of *Destructive Emotions: How Can We Overcome Them?, A Scientific Dialogue with the Dalai Lama*. Recent, significant research by three American brain scientists substantiated that deep meditation alters the state of the mind. Their historic experiment with SPECT technology (Single Photon Emission Computed Tomography, a high-tech imaging camera) which detects movements in the brain, used a subject who is an adept in Buddhist meditation. It provided evidence of the remarkable results of deep meditation. The subject maintained that whenever he entered into deep meditation, he always felt wholly and inextricably united with the infinite universe; the finite universe disappeared. The cessation of activity in the orientation association area of his brain proved that the brain responds to the infinite Reality as well as to finite reality. According to Andrew Newberg:

> . . . we had uncovered solid evidence that the mystical experiences of our subjects—the altered states of mind they described as the absorption of the self into something

larger—were not the result of emotional mistakes or mere wishful thinking, but were associated instead with a series of observable neurological events, which, while unusual, are not outside the range of normal brain function. In other words, mystical experience is biologically, observably, and scientifically real. (Andrew Newberg, *Why God Won't Go Away*, 2001, p. 7)

## THE KIRLIAN EFFECT

India's ancient seers called the subtle body, which is made up of the energy or light of the Soul, *Sukshma Sharira*. The principle of life in the embodied individual soul, *Jivatman*, is apart from the psycho-neurological physical body. That the subtle body with its characteristic aura is seen only in living, not dead forms of life, proves its existence as the foundation of the entire physical body with all its functions. In the West, advanced scientific research documented precise effects caused by every organic function of the human body on the aura of the body and called it the "Kirlian Effect." The effects on the aura enable the early diagnosis of disease in every human organ before the disease becomes apparent on traditional scanning and radiological equipment. Research using Kirlian technology is gaining acceptance in the West. According to *The New Soviet Psychic Discoveries*:

The work on the Kirlian effects' diagnostic properties alone is being conducted not only in Russia but in Rumania, Bulgaria, Hungary, Czechoslovakia and East Germany by over 1,000 high-level scientists, physicists, biologists, and medical doctors, with a total staff of as many as 50,000 laboratory assistants. (Swami Jagadatmananda, *Gospel of the Life Sublime* [Singapore, 1998], p. 152)

Modern Kirlian technology also evaluates the degree to which individuals can control and direct their energy through deep meditation. This is gradually leading to greater acceptance in the West of the extraordinary powers latent in the mind. Famed neurologist and skilled neurosurgeon Dr. Wilder Penfield summarized the extent of his scientific research in the book, *Secret of Mind*. In it, he advances his opinion that the West should recognize the independent function of the mind. He challenges the accepted view in the West that mind is dependent on the brain (Ibid., p. 153). This has specific relevance to the problem of unrestrained emotions.

## AUTHORITY OVER POWERFUL EMOTIONS

Emotions are as factual as germs; the emotional "viruses" of fear, hate, antagonism and the like can burrow deep into the subconscious mind and remain there for a lifetime. Control of the subconscious through the conscious will that is the result of meditation may alleviate them. A spiritual mind is based on strong, healthy nerves. All authentic schools of Yoga founded on Patanjali's teachings stabilize, integrate and unify the three powers of thought, will and emotions by strengthening the mind and the entire nervous system through concentration and meditation. Because intuition also comes into play, we eventually recognize and understand the causes and remedy of mental tension. Keeping a steady watch over the wandering habit of the mind helps us detect the source of our mental troubles and restlessness. With spiritual insight, all imagined or exaggerated symptoms of illness cease.

In his essay, "Philosophy of the Body: A New Approach to the Body Problem from Western and Indian Philosophies," D. M. Datta affirms:

The body is, again, the barometer of emotion[s], particularly the violent ones which warm, chill, shake, and strain the body. We can feel these conditions of the body directly. By successful control and pacification of anger, jealousy, ill will, greed, etc., not only the mind but also the body can be put at ease. So "bodily ease" is described by Buddha as one of the results of deeper concentration (*jnana* or *dhyana*) attained after the overcoming of all passions. . . . the control of [the] automatic nervous system claimed by the yogins and similar things show that we can increase our conscious control over the body to a large extent, though we may not fully control the body as some yogins claim to be able to do. The influence . . . of auto-suggestion in respect of one's own life . . . would seem also to suggest that the conscious will can, by some intense effort, sink into the unconscious level of life so as to work in a desired but unperceived way. (*Radhakrishnan: Comparative Studies in Philosophy Presented in Honour of His Sixtieth Birthday*, London / New York, 1968, pp. 324-6 passim)

Leading journals of psychiatry and medicine regularly publish professional articles, reports and long-term studies proving the broad ravages of disease; many diseases were previously unverified.

We are closely linked to our morbid thoughts. According to Dr. Robert Adler at the University of Rochester Medical School, "There is little question that we can alter the cause of disease by manipulating psychological factors." This and other similar opinions led to the idea that if negative emotions can cause illness, then positive emotions might stimulate wellness. Norman Cousins convincingly illustrates this point of view by introducing laughter as a powerful weapon to fight disease in his well-known book, *Anatomy of an Illness*. In 1964, doctors confirmed that a comprehensive illness, which Cousins had contracted in Russia, was irreversible and crippling. Recovery was highly improbable. The great power of his will to live made him adopt a hopeful outlook. He selected a cheerful environment, and in a self-prescribed course of action, Cousins carefully planned "the full exercise of the affirmative emotions as a factor in enhancing body chemistry." With help from his doctors, he healed himself. For the most part, he tapped into the healing power within his body through various methods that induced the "full force" of massive doses of laughter in him. He watched funny movies and asked his nurse to read him humorous books. Cousins maintained that a sustained jolly mood made him happy, which in turn alleviated his entire body and mind from pain and depression. His personal testimony in *Anatomy of an Illness* made the book a groundbreaking work in the area of physiological well-being.

Scientific data backs his theory with evidence that laughter increases respiration, which oxidizes the blood. To his credit, Cousins was the first to use and introduce to others the innovative therapy of strengthening the entire human organism and lifting the human spirit not through external exercise but through "inner jogging," or the exercise of mirth. Anxiety, depression, stress, anger, fears and phobias are all greatly purified by laughter, which reduces or eliminates their force. If we cannot accept a spiritual solution for these conditions, we can humorously daze our powerful emotions through paradoxical intention.

## *TAKING THE WIND OUT OF THE SAILS OF FEAR: PARADOXICAL INTENTION*

Immanuel Kant defined humour as "an affection arising from a strained expectation being suddenly reduced to nothing." In his book, *The Individual and His Religion,* Gordon Allport wrote, "The neurotic who learns to laugh at himself may be on the way to self-management, perhaps to a cure" (Quoted from *The Doctor and the Soul,* p. 209). Allport's statement has been broadly validated by the experience of patients in observable clinical conditions. In psychiatry, the phrase "paradoxical intention" indicates the clinical experience of mental therapists that validates both of these statements. We know that many people suffer from neurotic phobias—they expect what they fear the most will actually happen. They are suffering from "anticipatory anxiety."

In paradoxical intention, the therapist suggests to the patient to practise intending the feared event. Many patients who initially express lack of faith in this method, are cured of their phobias in the end, given that they succeed not *because of* but in *spite of,* the suggestion. Replacing the fear with the paradoxical wish takes the power out of the phobia. This has been observed clinically in patients, some of whom learned to laugh at themselves and their phobic obsessions.

Some physicians believe that the strong use of suggestion in paradoxical intention identifies it as one of the persuasive methods used by psychiatrists. It is true that persuasion is sometimes used prior to introducing paradoxical intention to the patient, when it is needed. However, Dr. Hans O. Gerz, the therapist in the cases presented below, explains:

> As a matter of fact, paradoxical intention is the exact opposite of persuasion, since it is not suggested that the patient simply suppress his fears (by the rational conviction that they are groundless) but, rather, that he overcome them by exaggerating them! (Ibid., p. 220).

> The patient suffering from obsessive-compulsive neurosis can, with this technique [paradoxical intention] recover or at least be greatly relieved. (Ibid., p. 228)

Of the many examples of paradoxical intention in Viktor Frankl's *The Doctor and the Soul*, two are cited here. In one case, a thirty-five-year-old man suffered from two phobias: he feared he would die from a heart attack and feared that he would never be able to sleep. The insightful Dr. Gerz asked his patient to "try as hard as possible" to die of a heart attack and "try to remain awake" every time each of these phobias troubled him. The patient began to laugh at his own neurotic symptoms. Laughter in turn lightened his mood and he followed the advice sincerely. In three days, both phobias were gone and had not appeared four weeks later when he reported himself fully cured (Ibid., p. 216).

Dr. Gerz also treated a twenty-nine-year-old mother of three with a long and painful history of multiple phobias and panic disorder. He told her to wish very hard for every phobia to become a reality. Though she had suffered much, the humour in this did not escape her. Her meticulous struggle and faithful participation in this instruction of paradoxical intention, together with medication, cured her of each phobia. Two years later, she was still phobia-free and leading a happy and normal family life (Ibid., p. 225).

## USING THE CREATIVE FACULTY

The creative faculty within us can offer life-saving curative energy. Many famous playwrights, writers, artists and the like testify to their uniquely intensive creative pursuits during periods of melancholy, depression, stress and anxiety. Alfred Bernhard Nobel (1833-1896) was an inventor, philanthropist and founder of the Nobel Prize. He attained great wealth by using his brilliant intellect and skill to create many inventions in addition to the dynamite for which he is famous. Three hundred and fifty-five of his inventions were patented by several governments. He was also a master financier, manager, and salesman, and learned half a dozen languages.

In spite of his great success, Nobel suffered bouts of depression that isolated him. "This insanity," he once wrote to a later love interest, "has been going on for seven years now, useless for you and exacting for me. It has embittered and wasted my life. I wish to devote my time to my work, to science, and I look upon women, all and sundry, young and old, as encroachers who steal my time" (Bradford Smith, *Men of Peace* [Philadelphia & New York], p. 192). In spite of this attitude, he strove to give his negative emotions a positive expression. According to Dr. Lawrence K. Altman, "Nobel was ill much of his life, experiencing migraine headaches, bouts of deep depression and, in his last few years, the chest pains of angina from blocked coronary arteries. . . . Nobel often relieved his depression by writing fiction, drama and poetry, which probably explains his interest in the literature prize [the other prizes are for medicine, chemistry and physics, peace and economics]" (*The New York Times*, September 26, 2006, p. F6).

## THREE FAMOUS PERSONALITIES

Melancholy produces lethargy and stagnation, and in its extreme form, a crippling lack of self-confidence. The three famous personalities below, removed their depression and sorrow by choosing to persevere in their creative labours by applying the positive values of endurance, hopeful optimism and resilience. Due to ill health, novelist A. J. Cronin was forced to abandon his profession as a doctor when he was only thirty-three and go to a peaceful location in Scotland. Deprived of all activity, he decided to try his hand at writing a novel, something he had longed to do for some time. *Hatter's Castle* progressed enthusiastically at first. However, he was undisciplined and unskilled in his new career as a writer. One line or paragraph would take him hours to compose, making him lose his self-confidence. He felt miserable at the thought of his ineptness and frustrated by his sincere desire to produce a novel worthy of his thoughts that people would like to read. In a moment of insanity, he threw away the manuscript he had laboured so hard to produce in the garbage. Then, thinking the matter was resolved and feeling quite sane, he went for a walk in drizzling rain. He happened to come upon a local farmer he knew. Old Angus was laboriously ditching a small area of bog in the hope of producing a pasture someday—something his father had also done but to no avail. With dogged resolution, however, Angus persevered. Seeing the farmer's utter lack of resentment at the difficulties he faced and his unquestioning faith in the outcome, the young Cronin, remorseful and furious with his recent lack of self-determination, went back to the garbage and retrieved his manuscript. Without becoming attached to the results of his effort, like the farmer from whom he had learned the lesson, he refused to be cowed by self-doubt and practised perseverance. The optimistic value he applied to his renewed writing effort benefited him as a writer and he regained his health as well. *Hatter's Castle*, a Book Society selection, was dramatized, serialized, translated into nineteen languages, bought by Hollywood and has sold over three million copies to date. His many other works are similarly appreciated.

"Every crucial experience can be regarded as a setback—or the start of a new kind of development." With this philosophy, novelist Mary Roberts Rinehart, whose books people everywhere love, faced cancer. When the diagnosis came in the spring of 1936, she summoned her courage, faith, and will to survive and began writing that autumn. Feeling strongly that fear, silence and delayed action cause many cancer deaths annually, she understood that "recovery often involves for the patient a complete mental and physical re-education." Demonstrating endurance, resilience and hope, she never betrayed her conviction that her healthy state would be restored. She never abandoned these values and continued to use her creative faculty. She completed her fifty-eighth novel eleven years after her diagnosis. Her message, "Face your danger with courage and faith, and with the will to survive," is based on the higher values of life.

Combining the power of thought and imagination with these higher values, sorrowful hearts are transformed. People everywhere are familiar with the verses of Longfellow's poems. One in particular engages us here. Longfellow long mourned the loss of his wife as a young man. Her loving memory still haunted him when he was a young professor at Harvard. Though life had become an empty dream for him, he knew he could not remain in that dejected, unbearable state. Hearing "a voice from my inmost heart, when I was rallying from depression," his inspired poem, "A Psalm of Life," came forth spontaneously:

> Tell me not in mournful numbers,
> Life is but an empty dream!—
> For the soul is dead that slumbers,
> And things are not what they seem.
>
> Life is real!  Life is earnest!
> And the grave is not its goal;
> Dust thou art, to dust returnest,
> Was not spoken of the soul.
>
> Not enjoyment, and not sorrow,
> Is our destined end or way;

But to act, that each tomorrow
      Find us farther than today.

Art is long, and Time is fleeting,
      And our hearts, though stout and brave,
Still, like muffled drums, are beating
      Funeral marches to the grave.

In the world's broad field of battle,
      In the bivouac of Life,
Be not like dumb, driven cattle!
      Be a hero in the strife!

Trust no Future, howe'er pleasant!
      Let the dead Past bury its dead!
Act, —act in the living Present!
      Heart within, and God o'erhead!

Lives of great men all remind us
      We can make our lives sublime,
And, departing, leave behind us
      Footprints on the sands of time;

Footprints, that perhaps another,
      Sailing o'er life's solemn main,
A forlorn and shipwrecked brother,
      Seeing, shall take heart again.

Let us, then, be up and doing,
      With a heart for any fate;
Still achieving, still pursuing,
      Learn to labor and to wait.

His unmistakably heartfelt lines of hope and faith went straight to the hearts of millions of ordinary people and students throughout the world, who read it and memorized it in nearly every major language, including Sanskrit.

## HIGHER VALUES OF ENDURANCE, HOPE AND RESILIENCE

Strong religious faith helps us to overcome pain and suffering. Experienced anthropologist Dr. James Freeman had intimate knowledge of the religion and culture of Orissa and personally witnessed some twenty-five persons walking over hot coals, most of them without pain or damage to the skin of their feet. The barefooted fire-walkers were demonstrating their innate faith in the protective force of Kali, the Hindu deity. "I have twice visited one community", Dr. Freeman says, "in which the main attraction involves walking three times over a path of burning coal over 180 feet long." This is not a ritual of endurance or manly indifference to pain. The psychological explanation behind this feat is their own purity and their strong faith in Kali. Unfortunately, as the poet observed, "We would rather be ruined than changed; we would rather die in our dread than climb the cross of the moment and let our illusions die" (W. H. Auden, *The Age of Anxiety*).

The higher values of endurance, hope and resilience comprise a spiritual attitude that assists our creative faculty when we are confronting life's inevitable pain and sorrow. Hindu scriptures want us to look upon suffering as *tapas*, austerity, which is an aid to spiritual insight. The *Brihadaranyaka Upanishad* (V. 11. 1) declares that calm submission to God brings a peaceful acceptance of suffering that is equivalent to practising religious austerities. We must learn to endure everything for the sake of higher knowledge, which alone brings us joy. In order to enjoy that future brightness, we must endure the pain and think of our body as an instrument for seeking and attaining spiritual joy, not as a receptacle of purposeless suffering.

Logotherapy conveys the same message, that one is able to endure suffering because of a deep, abiding faith in the higher meaning and purpose of human life. "A man's concern, even his despair, over the worthwhileness of life is a *spiritual distress* but by no means a mental disease" ((*Man's Search for Meaning*, p. 163). That positive idea allows us to put up with all difficulties. The blessedness of life comes to those who have undergone suffering heroically and optimistically, although some pass through their ordeals with stoicism, indifferently submissive to natural law. It is out of faith that endurance comes.

One requires a glimpse of the horrific conditions of the concentration camp experience that Viktor Frankl described in his books in order to appreciate the moral strength of the individuals who, in spite of their awful experiences in the camps, never lost their strong conviction of soul-consciousness, meaning and purpose of life. They emerged from the camps greatly strengthened, though physically scarred. Frankl writes:

And again, what happened on our arrival in that camp [Dachau], after a journey lasting two days and three nights? There had not been enough room for everybody to crouch on the floor of the carriage at the same time. The majority of us had to stand all the way, while a few took turns at squatting on the scanty straw which was soaked with human urine. When we arrived the first important news that we heard from older prisoners was that this comparatively small camp (its population was 2,500) had no "oven," no crematorium, no gas! . . . This joyful surprise put us all in a good mood. The wish of the senior warden in our hut in Auschwitz had come true: we had come, as quickly as possible, to a camp which did not have a "chimney"—unlike Auschwitz. We laughed and cracked jokes in spite of, and during, all we had to go through in the next few hours.

When we new arrivals were counted, one of us was missing. So we had to wait outside in the rain and cold wind until the missing man was found. He was at last discovered in a hut, where he had fallen asleep from exhaustion. Then the roll call was turned into a punishment parade. All through the night and into the next morning, we had to stand outside, frozen and soaked to the skin after the strain of our long journey. And yet we were all very pleased! There was no chimney in this camp and Auschwitz was a long way off. (*Man's Search for Meaning*, pp. 70-2)

Under indescribably cruel conditions, these camp inmates avoided despair and came to understand from the depth of their soul that the meaning of life entailed more than their individual cycle of life and death. They were "smelted and shaped" by their suffering to embrace a vaster scope, a greater vision of life's meaning and purpose:

Once the meaning of suffering had been revealed to us, we refused to minimize or alleviate the camp's tortures by ignoring them or harboring false illusions and entertaining artificial optimism. Suffering had become a task on which we did not want to turn our backs. We had realized its hidden opportunities for achievement, . . . (*Man's Search for Meaning*, p. 124)

Even individuals with a delicate constitution withstood the strain better than others who were more vigorous. With all its horrors and brutalities, the Nazi concentration camps may have been a place where inmates cultivated a spirit of detachment that protected them from later emotional scars. Spiritually oriented inmates with some degree of detachment were relatively unaffected by their own suffering and the terrible circumstances surrounding them. In this way, they avoided a partial or complete breakdown of spirit. Torture is not perceived as torture, and pain is avoided, when suffering is faced with supreme tolerance and spiritual, psychological and emotional adjustment to such conditions.

Principled logotherapists indeed offer a unique opportunity of self-transcendence to the patient:

> The logotherapist's role consists in widening and broadening the visual field of the patient so that the whole spectrum of meaning and values becomes conscious and visible to him. Logotherapy does not need to impose any judgments on the patient, for, actually, truth imposes itself and needs no intervention. . . . For only to the extent to which man commits himself to the fulfillment of his life's meaning, to this extent he also actualizes himself. In other words, self-actualization cannot be attained if it is made an end in itself, but only as a side effect of self-transcendence. (*Man's Search for Meaning*, pp. 174-5)

There is an intimate psychological relationship between one's attitude and one's suffering. Those who are dedicated themselves to noble causes always exhibit extraordinary moral courage in times of crisis. Suffering affects the mind. If the mind calmly faces the consequences, however unjustified, with serenity that is born of moral purity, it remains undisturbed. Wounded soldiers evacuated from the battlefield are so relieved to be released from the front lines and so anticipate reunion with their families that they often experience little or no pain in spite of severe wounds. Their wounds signify the certainty of a more secure emotional, economic and physical life distant from the spectre of war. Civilians, on the other hand, anxiously consider themselves incapacitated, financially threatened and deformed by serious injuries and react differently. The difference in attitudes demonstrated by the wounded soldier and the injured civilian illustrates the different qualities of suffering. A soldier with a severe wound may deny having pain but may then complain loudly and bitterly when the hypodermic needle pierces him in the relative safety of his home. The attitude of the mind plays a vital role in the perception of feeling.

## ARE WE "ENGINEERED" FOR RELIGIOUS FAITH?

Even with the current resurgence of public service by faith-based organizations and its approval by powerful politicians, modern medicine still fails to appreciate fully our innate desire to discover our true, inner spiritual identity. Physicians and researchers alike are unduly cautious about faith in their attempt to minimize the risk of appearing unscientific in their approach to healing. Yet since the 1960s, America's passion for an immediate, transcendent experience of God has increased. Major polls indicate increased religious tolerance and spiritual interest virtually across the religious spectrum. Some newly constructed churches seat as many as 16,000 worshippers per service (*The Business Week*, May 23, 2005).

Evangelical preachers wield tremendous political power today. Two-thirds of Americans claim to pray daily, another third, to meditate. These facts point to America's apparent, though heavily disguised, renewed spiritual need. There are many deceptive signs of popular disavowal of God and general sacrilege driven by the media. Despite these visibly superficial attempts to make the sacred profane and inauthentic, there is a genuine desire to know the truth that frees us from all that is false and pretentious.

In his book, *Timeless Healing*, Dr. Herbert Benson proposes that we are engineered for religious faith: "Our genetic blueprint has made believing in an Infinite Absolute part of our nature." He suggests that evolution has equipped us with a mechanism to compensate for our uniquely human capacity to ponder our own mortality: "To counter this fundamental angst, humans are also wired for God." He based his premise on a five-year study of patients battling chronic illnesses with meditation. Patients who reported feeling closer to God while meditating experienced quicker recoveries and better health. According to Dr. Benson, "Faith in the medical treatment [is] wonderfully therapeutic, successful in treating 60% to 90% of the most common medical problems. But if you so believe, faith in an invincible and infallible force carries even more healing power . . . It is a supremely potent belief."

The basic, supportive societal role of churches and temples also serves to maintain the general health of its members. In one nine-year study of mortality rates among 4,700 men and women, a higher death rate existed of unmarried men as well as of men who did not belong to any religious organization, or who were socially isolated. On the other hand, among women, marital status played no role at all, while church and group membership and friendliness towards others gave them a lowered mortality rate (L. F. Berman and S. L. Syme, "Social Networks, Host Resistance, and Mortality: A Nine-year Follow-up of Alameda County residents," *American Journal of Epidemiology* 109: 186-204, 1979).

## *HEALING POWER OF PRAYER*

A *TIME*/CNN poll of 2,004 Americans taken in 1996 found that 82% believed in the healing power of prayer and 64% believed that doctors should pray with patients who ask them to do so. Dr. David Larson notes that less than two-thirds of doctors believe in God, and expresses their general view: "We physicians are culturally insensitive about the role of religion. It is very important to many of our pat ents and not important to lots of doctors." If doctors do not improve or re-examine this view, patients who rely on them for broader medical treatment will continue to feel isolated, fearful and insecure. Fear is the worst form of mental suffering, whether it is physical fear, or psychological fear and therefore existential.

Generally, as some of the case studies previously cited have shown, most illnesses have emotional components that can be healed through prayerfulness. Illness and antisocial behaviour in some individuals masquerade as a "solution" to their unbearable distress. Some cancer patients are desperate to learn the reason why normal cells betrayed their immune systems—although it is known that a lost zest for life has the potential to weaken the immune system. Miraculous drugs often have no healing effect. One doctor addressed a medical assembly with these words:

> As an alienist, and one whose whole life has been concerned with the sufferings of the mind, I would state that all of the hygienic measures to counteract disturbed sleep, depression of spirits and all the miserable sequels of a distressed mind, I would undoubtedly give the first place to the simple habit of prayer. (Dr. Hysop in his address to a medical congress, quoted in *The Power of Prayer*, p. 180. Quoted from A. R. Wadia, *Religion as a Quest for Values* [Calcutta, 1950], pp. 26-7)

There is great constructive spiritual imagination associated with prayer. Repeating the prayer of a great saint is one way to connect with the spiritual power and experience of the saint. Repeating the prayer brings a healthy peacefulness to the mind and body.

AA teaches its practitioners to recite and meditate upon the familiar Prayer of St. Francis, which they have adopted in the following words to achieve success in the eleventh of AA's Twelve Steps:

> *Lord, make me a channel of thy peace—that where there is hatred, I may bring love; that where there is wrong, I may bring the spirit of forgiveness; that where there is discord, I may bring harmony; that where there is error, I may bring truth; that where there is doubt, I may bring faith; that where there is despair, I may bring hope; that where there are shadows, I may bring light; that where there is sadness, I may bring joy. Lord, grant that I may seek rather to comfort than to be comforted; to understand, than to be understood; to love, than to be loved. For it is by self-forgetting that one finds. It is by forgiving that one is forgiven. It is by dying that one awakens to Eternal Life. Amen.*

Spiritual living gives us compassionate understanding, optimism, moral strength, and above all, assures us of the eternal nature of our Soul. Fear is promoted solely by the lack of spiritual living. We cannot shed light on fear and suffering without spiritual armour.

## LIGHT ON FEAR AND SUFFERING

According to one well-respected psychologist, "Fear is the most disintegrating enemy of human personality" and "worry is the most subtle and destructive of all human diseases." American surgeon Dr. George W. Crile confirms this point of view: "We fear not only in our minds but in our hearts, brains and viscera, so that whatever the cause of the fear and the worry, the effect can always be noted in the cells, tissues and organs of the body." Recognizing the American epidemic of fear and worry, another physician says, "All doctors are having cases of illness which are brought on directly by fear, and aggravated by worry and a feeling of insecurity." Yet another doctor provides his insight on the role of spiritual faith in this regard:

> A Viennese doctor, Dr. Hans Finsterer, who believes "the unseen hand of God" helps make an operation successful, was selected by the International College of Surgeons for its highest honor, "Master of Surgery." He was cited for his work in abdominal surgery with the use of local anesthesia only. . . . [Dr. Finsterer says,] "When we are once again convinced of the importance of God's help in our activities, and especially in the treatment of our patients, then true progress will have been accomplished in restoring the sick to health." (*The Power of Positive Thinking*, p. 187-8)

When we feel inadequate to cope with life's problems, we react with fear, due to the absence of a spiritually guided life and values. There are many types of rational and irrational fear. Rational fear accompanies any immediate threat to life or limb; like a cobra, it strikes and retreats quickly. Human emotions that cause us to react to real or imagined events fuel irrational fears and make us feel inferior. There is also emotional fear and spiritual fear. Like a deep, central current rising to the surface, fear moves from the mind and heart to the body's periphery. It does not appear out of nowhere. It comes from an egocentric mind that relates to external or internal forces.

If we selfishly anticipate a short-term gain or loss, a survival or defeat, it affects our interpretation of facts.

Reactions are usually conscious, rarely unconscious, and pervade our entire organism—lips quiver, limbs quake, nerves twitch, the blood races or comes to a sluggish halt. In extreme fear, the brain, emotions and limbs "freeze." In this state, we cannot reason and mobilize the senses to our rescue. The abundant restless energy gathered in the "engine" of the mind does not know in which direction it should go. We usually react with a "fight or flight" attitude. American psychiatrist Karl Menninger treated the subject of our reactive states and their relevance to a poised, integrated personality. In his book, *You and Psychiatry*, Menninger wrote:

> Our failures are expressed in one of two types of reaction: flight or attack. Both these reactions indicate instability. Sometimes we want to run away from everything that troubles; self-induced sickness and drunkenness are such expressions of flight. If they are not cured, personality degenerates. The *attack* reaction, if properly directed, may bring readjustment resulting in more or less complete poise. Through the right kind of fighting spirit, learning to fight the enemies within, we may attain a measure of poise and peace.

An overactive mind absorbed in fear usually accompanies an under-active body. As one observer wrote, "People generate fears while they sit and overcome them when they move" (*The Rediscovery of Man*, p. 103). Today's nuclear family with its increased leisure actually cultivates fear through excessive brooding, thinking, talking, and media's absorption in violence. Many resort to lengthy self-analysis. All these are counterproductive and destroy our peace of mind. Laziness, inertness and self-absorption also generate fear. Laziness is not relaxation. Even when we are working, lower thoughts can still occupy the mind. We may good-naturedly recall that we once aired and resolved our troubles and anxieties more naturally in days gone by—women gathered to wash, sew and cook; men gathered to repair and build, etc. The truth is that whether we work or not, the mind occupied with higher thoughts is purified. It is a spiritually creative, dynamic form of mental relaxation, which makes us perform beneficial actions.

Fear has an existential as well as a physiological cause. It is ubiquitous and encompassing—sometimes it is recognizable, sometimes its cause is unknown. In its grip, we sink further into moral weakness, instability and dishonesty. We may exhibit alternate moods of hysteria, stubbornness, darkness, ambivalence, despair and weeping—in short, we are undone to the core. We rally quickly to disguise our fear with bravado, pretence, aloofness, fanatical zeal or martyrdom. Fear presents us with a vicious, unnatural cycle of confusion. A wildly imaginative, undisciplined and confused mind cannot comprehend truth. It lacks wisdom about the goal of life and the way to happiness.

We misuse our talents by immersing them day and night solely to satisfy ordinary human desires. There is no fault in being diligent about our physical appearance, food and diet, comforts and entertainment, etc. However, what are we doing in addition to make ourselves fearless, more dignified and capable of adjusting to others without finding fault in them? These common issues demand our attention and a spiritual answer. The following narrative illustrates a typical case of anxiety and its spiritual solution:

A young woman of thirty years of age had enjoyed a fairly happy married life until the depression of the early thirties. At that time, her husband's financial security was threatened. Then her very successful father-in-law died. This woman was apprehensive lest her widowed mother-in-law should request help from the husband. The mother-in-law appeared in the picture, which created serious tension in the young wife. She had a nervous breakdown and all the symptoms of serious mental disorder. She was stabilized by attaining a higher philosophy of life. She realized that the mother-in-law would not be a burden to her, even if worse came to worst. She was also convinced that the life of consecration can alone remove her egocentric, selfish attitude. It took several months for her to establish herself in this new way of thinking. In the meantime, she systematically went through spiritual exercises of concentration, meditation, and so forth, and gradually developed will power. (Swami Akhilananda, *Mental Health and Hindu Psychology* [New York, 1951], p. 91.)

"Sow a thought and you reap an act. Sow an act and you reap a habit. Sow a habit and you reap a character. Sow a character and you reap a destiny." This axiom emphasizes that we are not victims of destiny. To some extent, both self-effort through spiritual living and strength of will to do good, mitigate our bad karma.

When we transgress moral principles, guilt and remorse prick our conscience. The mind is no longer calm. Mental disease follows. Any one of us can conjure up numerous common scenarios of stress and anxiety. We have all readily observed how the normal mood suddenly changes and the symptoms of frustration, resentment, jealousy, and anger appear. Though the tense atmosphere affects everyone, these inevitable events are instructive from a spiritual perspective. If we accept the fact that there is disappointment and frustration in life, we can give greater attention to what is more important and less attention to what is less important, without being careless, ungenerous or unfair.

We have only to recognize that habitual culprit—egoism—with its impulsive, self-centred and unsympathetic behaviour. We cannot afford to think of ourselves merely as creatures of habit. Everyone benefits when we choose to transform bad habits into good ones. Swami Vivekananda says:

> It is said, "Habit is second nature," it is first nature also, and the whole nature of man; everything that we are is the result of habit. That gives us consolation, because, if it is only habit, we can make and unmake it at any time . . . The only remedy for bad habits is counter habits; all the bad habits that have left their impressions are to be controlled by good habits. Go on doing good, thinking holy thoughts continuously; that is the only way to suppress base impressions. Never say any man is hopeless, because he only represents a character, a bundle of habits, which can be checked by new and better ones. Character is repeated habits, and repeated habits alone can reform character. (*C. W.*, I: 207-8)

The remedy for a fearful mind is to acquire a true understanding of spiritual life. Life is God. God being the mine of our spiritual strength, we should support all our actions with a deep conviction of our connection to God. This positive aspect of religion sustains inner spiritual life and gives us a sense of security and strength. Unspiritual thoughts and habits sustain fear and sorrow; we can solve all our problems if we shift our attention to something higher. Our fears and neuroses will definitely disappear.

Spiritual values are dynamic, not static; their full, fiery power transforms our mind. Our lives change for the better when we face life's challenges in the spirit of true religion. When we improve the mind, we demonstrate that we are cultivating mental broadness, acceptance, and expansion of heart. Our improved quality of mind is verified as soon as we become aware that the world is unreal. The Vedic prayer says, "Lead us from the unreal to the Real, from darkness to Light, from death to Immortality" (*Brihadaranyaka Upanishad*, I. 3. 28). The Real is Eternal, Infinite, Imperishable Purity and Bliss.

Placing our total faith and confidence in an impermanent, ever-changing, perishable world cannot provide us with real happiness. The fearful global consequences of our spiritual, ethical and moral lapses are bearing down upon us. Swami Vivekananda's dictum, "There is no limit to the power of the human mind," supports an integrated, holistic approach to overall health guided by the innate divine Power in man. A votary of spiritual values is a dynamic beneficial source of strength and inspiration to all. The divinity we cultivate in ourselves liberates others from ignorance and fear.

# 4

# PRACTICAL SPIRITUAL PRINCIPLES TO ALLEVIATE STRESS

*My child, if you want peace, then do not look into anybody's faults. Look into your own faults. Learn to make the world your own. No one is a stranger, my child; the whole world is your own.*

—Holy Mother Sarada Devi's
final message to suffering humanity

*Men will wrangle for religion, write for it, fight for it, die for it, anything but live for it.*

—Charles Colton (*1780-1832*)

We begin to alleviate stress when we recognize that all problems are created by thought and deeds and begin in the mind. Our reaction to them leads to stress. Stress and doubt exist subjectively in the mind; they have no valid objective existence. We live to fulfil endless desires that do not bring us lasting joy and peace.

A life without meaning has never been helpful to the human race. We must have conviction in the higher meaning of life if we are to avoid unnecessary worry and stress. In his autobiography, Tolstoy made this poignant observation:

Search among these people for a man, poor or rich, for whom what he earns secures what he considers necessary according to the world's teaching, and you will find one in a thousand. Everyone struggles with his whole strength to obtain what he does not need but what is demanded for him by the teaching of the world, and the absence of which therefore makes him unhappy. And as soon as he obtains what is required, something else, and again something else, is demanded of him, and so this work of Sisyphus continues endlessly, ruining the life of man. . . . They all have more and more to burden their already over-laden life with work, and devote their life and soul entirely to the service of the world's teaching. . . . But perhaps the life itself during which a man does all this is happy? (Leo Tolstoy, *A Confession and What I Believe* [London, 1927], pp. 305-6)

## HELPFUL FUNDAMENTAL TEACHINGS

The common troubles of human life do not exist among the sub-human species. Unlike them, we react subjectively to circumstances and tend to fret over them. We must accept five inevitable and unavoidable facts: (1) fullness of youth gives way to old age; (2) disease will come; (3) death will come; (4) everything dear to us is subject to change, decay and separation; (5) we reap the fruits of our thoughts and actions, good and bad.

No one can escape these facts. To accept them and to apply certain basic principles strengthens us to develop peace of mind. Five active principles are relevant. We must (1) lead an ethical life; (2) fulfill our duty conscientiously and lovingly, to the best of our ability; (3) attach the greatest importance to a cherished noble ideal that gives life meaning; (4) have unshakable faith in ourselves, the innate goodness of others, and God; (5) strengthen our mind with spiritual thoughts.

Five passive principles also apply to which we must be receptive. They include (1) because God's will is always just, there is a higher purpose to suffering; (2) suffering is God's gift of compassion for our spiritual growth; (3) seek another's opinion before rushing to judgment; (4) capacities differ in mankind; each must manifest their own potential; (5) do not find fault with others; concentrate on your own faults. Both sets of principles help us avoid a false sense of contentment whenever things are going smoothly and we think that events are happening according to our own will. Making these valuable ethical principles a part of our daily life assures us of the treasure of a peaceful mind.

We deceive ourselves if we perceive objective conditions of life subjectively. There are many common self-deceptions. They include (1) comparing ourselves with others; (2) evaluating objective circumstances incorrectly; (3) being overly egoistic; (4) fulfiling never-ending desires; (5) magnifying imaginary troubles, (6) brooding over the past and future, and (7) feeling insecure.

There are practical, effective spiritual principles to resolve each of them: (1) correct identification and valuation, (2) correct occupation, (3) correct selectivity, (4) correct decisiveness, (5) correct activity, (6) correct spiritual faith, (7) correct dietary guidelines, (8) correct use of *Prana*, and (9) correct value of cheerfulness.

## BASIC SELF-DECEPTIONS

*(1) Comparing ourselves with others.* We foolishly believe that we best evaluate ourselves by comparing ourselves to others.

The root of the problem is that our desire for material things makes us react to ordinary, objective events. "The habit of thinking in terms of comparison is a fatal one" (Bertrand Russell). The eminent theologian Professor Joshua Loth Liebman, authored the best-selling book, *Peace of Mind*, during World War II. He wrote:

> A man may have a home, possessions, a charming family, and yet find all these things ashy to his taste because he has been outstripped in the marathon race by some other runners to the golden tape line. It is not that he does not possess enough for his wants but that others possess more. It is the *more* that haunts him, makes him deprecate himself, and minimize his real achievements. This is the cancer eating away at his serenity. . . . Psychology will help religion to diminish the worship of the golden calf among men as it aids men to become free of their over-excessive demands upon themselves. When, instead of the pathological race for more houses and jewels, cars and refrigerators, bonds and stocks . . . when, instead of seeking these fictitious goals, men learn a certain modesty about things and become genuinely contented with their real contributions and achievements—only then is serenity achieved. Only when we harness our own creative energies to *goals which are of our own adult choice*, not imposed on us by the compulsions of unresolved childhood competition, can we call ourselves mature and happy. (Quoted from *Light from Many lamps*, pp. 237-8)

The struggle for life is often nothing more than a competition for success. Bertrand Russell observed, "What people mean by the struggle for life is really the struggle for success. What people fear when they engage in the struggle is not that they will fail to get their breakfast the next morning, but that they will fail to outshine their neighbors" (*Conquest of Happiness*, p. 45). Bombardment from the media with tantalizingly glamorous but unrealistic views of life keeps us constantly engaged in this fruitless effort. Deprived of the stimulation, we feel bored, depressed and unfulfilled. We eventually lose the spontaneity and self-acceptance that healthy spiritual values generate in us. A very good way to improve ourselves in the school of life is to measure our own ability to follow goodness and develop our will power and dynamism, without comparing ourselves to others.

*(2) Evaluating objective circumstances incorrectly.* If we live aimlessly, we cannot evaluate even the most ordinary events correctly. Insignificant desires assume great importance in our mind, making us unhappy and restless. This represents our frustrated quest for spiritual meaning. Trite matters— selecting the wrong tie, unhappiness with our physical appearance, unexpected changes to our plans or missing some detail—can make us wholly miserable. Lack of objectivity and common sense destroys the peaceful foundation of life.

Though they clutter our busy lives, we should not inflate trite matters out of proportion. For example, a young couple, preparing over a week for an elaborate dinner at their home, obviously wish to please and impress their guests. At the end of the week, they are tired but happily anticipating a perfect evening. Just before the guests are to arrive, the wife discovers that the tablecloth and napkins do not match—a major detail to her. She reacts and immediately loses her joyous anticipation. Hysterical and upset over her disturbed sense of perfection, she tries desperately to correct the situation with the help of her local laundry, but it is too late—the guests are about to arrive. Feeling helpless and angry, she vents her frustration at her husband and starts an argument but he remains composed, since it is not as important to him. This makes her feel worse, which ruins the evening for her.

Another fastidious man prepares himself for work. He leaves the house feeling satisfied in his nice suit and spotless shirt and tie. At work, his boss notices that his tie does not go well with the rest of his attire and pleasantly makes a humorous remark about it. The young perfectionist cannot tolerate the slightest criticism. He feels humiliated and incompetent, an exaggerated response caused by his sense of inadequacy. Throughout the day, his boss's comment mercilessly eats away at him mentally. He still cannot let go of it when he gets home. He vents his frustration on his wife, children and the family dog. He is distraught over a minor incident. A similar event caused a humiliated famous writer to commit suicide.

*(3) Being overly egoistic.* Worldliness saps our divine qualities and inflates our ego, whose tell-tale sign is self-centredness. The individual is "ever-complaining that the world does not devote itself to making you happy" (George Bernard Shaw). "One's ego is no very large part of the world. The man who can center his thoughts and hopes upon something transcending self can find a certain peace in the ordinary troubles of life which is impossible to the pure egoist" (*The Conquest of Happiness*, p. 73). An unspiritual life gives greater emphasis to the ego.

*(4) Fulfiling never-ending desires.* Endless desires lead to endless restlessness and lack of fulfilment. Materialism creates tremendous stress at home and in the workplace. Driven by advertising, consumers yearn for new products. Corporations struggling to exceed their profit quotas and satisfy their financial greed spend billions predicting consumers' acquisitive habits with the help of marketing experts. They create fads that deliberately target and lure consumers to buy into the

deceptive belief that material possessions bring happiness, wealth and longevity. In a materialistic, consumerist society, demand exceeds ability. Struggling to acquire whatever we desire by working overtime, we sacrifice family life, relaxation and health and totally neglect the spiritual life. We are work-alcoholics unaware that the heart actually works fewer hours than we do. Dr. Walter B. Cannon of Harvard Medical School said, "Most people have the idea that the heart is working all the time. As a matter of fact, there is a definite rest period after each contraction. *When beating at a moderate rate of seventy pulses per minute, the heart is actually working only nine hours out of the twenty-four. In the aggregate its rest periods total a full fifteen hours per day"* (Dale Carnegie, *How to Stop Worrying and Start Living* [New York, 1984], p. 232).

Our every attempt to find happiness in pleasure and acquisitions is in vain. We are overworked and overindulged, battered by our own excesses, and injured to the core. Lacking awareness of immortality, the wounded soul seeks rest. Life never fully satisfies our insincere demands and impossible desires. The right desire of our inner spiritual nature seeks fulfilment in God alone.

*(5) Magnifying imaginary troubles.* An insecure, fearful mind projects imaginary forms and ideas upon ordinary forms and objective circumstances. When imagination runs wild in an undisciplined, unspiritual mind, it moves in circles, like a dog chasing its tail but with the added torment of improbable outcomes. For example, long before a future social event that we are planning takes place, we may imagine problems and worry about them. Bertrand Russell openly confessed his nervous tension and dread of public speaking. He overcame it by boldly confronting his weakness: "At first every audience terrified me, and nervousness made me speak very badly . . . I

always hoped I might break my leg before I had to make a speech, and when it was over I was exhausted from the nervous strain. Gradually, I taught myself to feel that it did not matter whether I spoke well or ill, the universe would remain much the same in either case" (*The Conquest of Happiness*, pp. 72-3). His experience teaches us to devote our energy to higher pursuits and to apply reason to our imagined worries and anxieties.

English novelist, critic and essayist Virginia Woolf (1882-1941) could not face the anxiety and lack of courage her imagination caused. Profoundly depressed by World War II, and fearing another nervous breakdown, she committed suicide. Her fulfiling marital and professional life did not prevent her from drowning herself. Facing our magnified imaginary worries and fear boldly and truthfully with reason lessens these symptoms of mental fatigue.

*(6) Brooding over the past and future.* Brooding over the irreversible past and imaginary future causes great distress and provides only temporary relief. It is useless to mull over the past and future, which do not exist in the present. We tend to glorify the mediocre consequences of past events and create a utopian future when we are anxious or depressed about present conditions. It is hard to maintain the pretence of these two impractical strategies. When the hollow fantasies dissolve, our pain and anguish increase. Unreality cannot give us freedom and peace. Swami Vivekananda says, ". . . when people cease to think of the past or future, when they give up the idea of body, because the body comes and goes and is limited, then they have risen to a higher ideal" (*C. W.*, II: 79).

*(7) Feeling insecure.* Without healthy spiritual values, people feel insecure. Stress and trauma huddle beneath the broad umbrella of insecurity. Every one of us will experience the

inevitable circumstances of the vast, unpredictable universe. Sudden or premature death, unexpected grave illness, loss of employment, epidemics and wars all take their toll on us. We may walk innocently or recklessly into harm's way or be cut off in our prime. For everyone's welfare, we must adjust our lives to meet these circumstances with courage and strength. Every unhappy event requires psychological, emotional and physical adaptation. Spirituality is the anchor of inner security. It gives us wisdom and depth with which to meet adversity's grave challenges. "Wisdom leads to forbearance, forbearance to further wisdom" (Spinoza).

## PRACTICAL, EFFECTIVE SPIRITUAL PRINCIPLES RESOLVE SELF-DECEPTIONS

*(1) Correct identification and valuation.* All problems are created in the mind and have a dual nature: external (presented to the mind) and internal (reactions in the mind). If we confront external events with ignorance, we disturb the innate peacefulness of the mind. External events and objects exist objectively—they are distinct from the mind. They appear on the mirror of the mind as do images on a blank movie screen. Objective identification permits truthful evaluation.

.Problems have a dual solution also. We must address external events and the mind that perceives them by concentrating on the facts objectively and dispassionately, as a witness. If we superimpose many thoughts on the matter, we will overreact. We must also understand the facts, think about them briefly and reasonably, and act effectively with discrimination. Our thought should be singular and vigorous, our action quick and affirmative. Correct identification valuation avoids extremes and replaces flawed values with spiritual ones.

*(2) Correct occupation.* Swamiji says, "Life is ever expanding, contraction is death. The self-seeking man who is looking after his personal comforts and leading a lazy life—there is no room for him even in hell" (*C. W.*, VI: 294). Alexis Carrel reflected on the subject of right conduct:

> Laziness does not only consist in doing nothing, in sleeping too long, in working badly or not at all, but also in devoting our leisure to stupid and useless things. Endless chattering, card playing, dancing, rushing about aimlessly in motorcars, abusing the cinema and the radio—all these reduce the intelligence. It is also dangerous to have a smattering of too many subjects without acquiring a real knowledge of any one. We need to defend ourselves against the rapidity of communication, by the number of magazines and newspapers, by the motorcar, the airplane and the telephone, to multiply to excess the number of ideas, feelings, things and people which enter into our daily lives. Carried beyond certain limits, specialization can be just as much an obstacle to spiritual development as too wide a field of interests. (*Reflections on Life*, pp. 104-5)

High thinking and plain living are the happiness and joy of a simple life.

*(3) Correct selectivity.* Life demands selectivity and scrutiny. Healthy lifestyles are based on spiritual culture. Spiritual life is simple and pure. All diversity is founded on spiritual unity and harmony. This is most evident in India, where God has been continuously worshipped as Mother since Vedic times and where the tradition of motherhood seeks to ensure the spiritual quality of successive generations. Deep thinkers in the West also recognize women's tremendous supportive role in society as wives and mothers:

The ideal which the wife and mother makes for herself, the manner in which she understands duty and life, contain the faith of the community. Her faith becomes the star of the conjugal ship, and her love the animating principle that fashions the future of all belonging to her. Woman is the salvation or destruction of the family. She carries its destinies in the folds of her mantle. (Henri F. Amiel, quoted from *Light from Many Lamps*, p. 252)

A virtuous life transmits the values of spiritual culture.

*(4) Correct decisiveness.* "Nothing is so exhausting as indecision, and nothing is so futile," said Bertrand Russell (*The Conquest of Happiness*, p. 72). Indecisiveness, doubt and passivity make us anxious, nervous and weak. We wait until the last moment to make wrong decisions—when it is too late to exercise reason and understanding. Wasteful thinking and indecision come from our inability to guide our mental energy along a fixed "track" of spiritual principles. A clear understanding and acceptance of basic human morals and ethics allows us to act decisively. Correct decisiveness does not trouble the mind or waste the vital energy that we should direct to our spiritual goals.

At the very least, as the saying goes, "a timely bad decision is better than no decision at all"—this effectively breaks the bad habit of indecisiveness. We should accept the risks of acting decisively and courageously when matters confront us. Poor decisions teach us profitable lessons as well as good ones.

*(5) Correct activity.* When problems consume our mind, we all feel the need to relax mentally and physically. If we do not turn, as many do, to cheap entertainment, physical exercise (walking, swimming, cycling, hiking, mountain climbing, Hatha Yoga, etc.) neutralizes our mental stress and physical

tension. The brief pause from our troubles that these activities provide can become lasting if we spiritualize them. Practical spiritual exercises give us mental poise.

Correct activity promotes health and leads to God-realization. Unity with the Divine fulfills the one desire that underlies all the other desires that hide it from our view—our need for unity with the all-loving Divine. Whether we are active or inactive, we can encourage our mind to dwell constantly in its spiritual dimension. We will be "touched by eternity," filled with joy and bliss and continue to live in the same world with correct understanding—our infatuation with it will disappear. Swamiji says:

> The individual's life is in the life of the whole, the individual's happiness is in the happiness of the whole; apart from the whole, the individual's existence is inconceivable—this is an eternal truth and is the bedrock on which the universe is built. To move slowly towards the infinite whole, bearing a constant feeling of intense sympathy and sameness with it, being happy with its happiness and being distressed in its affliction, is the individual's sole duty. (C. W., IV: 463)

A weak mind soaked in worldliness seeks material pleasures and strays from the real goal of life. A false sense of security and happiness ultimately robs us of inner spiritual freedom. Degenerative practices can seep into religious life; unknowingly, we become their slave. Swami Vivekananda says:

> Therefore, use your own minds, control body and mind yourselves, remember that until you are a diseased person, no extraneous will can work upon you; avoid everyone, however great and good he may be, who asks you to believe

blindly. All over the world there have been dancing and jumping and howling sects, who spread like infection when they begin to sing and dance and preach; they also are a sort of hypnotists. They exercise a singular control for the time being over sensitive persons, alas! often, in the long run, to degenerate whole races. Ay, it is healthier for the individual or the race to remain wicked than be made apparently good by such morbid extraneous control . . . Therefore, beware of everything that takes away your freedom. Know that it is dangerous, and avoid it by all the means in your power. (*C. W.*, I: 173)

We usually allow one sentiment to dominate over the others when we marshal our energy for activity. True religion advocates integrity of character. It transforms us by teaching us how to control the lower instincts and manifest our higher nature for the sake of spiritual freedom. Swami Vivekananda says that the more we conquer our lower nature and manifest our higher divine nature, the greater and more stable society will be. "It is a change of the soul itself for the better that alone will cure the evils of life." Daily systematic practice of spiritual principles strikes at the root of evil in society. It requires more than intellectual comprehension.

*(6) Correct spiritual faith.* Deep faith in spiritual ideals and spiritual living comes from a religious attitude. "I live, move and have my being in God," says St. Paul. Swamiji says, "Faith, faith, faith in ourselves, faith, faith in God—this is the secret of greatness" (*C. W.*, III: 190). Strong spiritual faith does not allow us to be shaken to our roots; we accept predicaments without resorting to hallucinogenic drugs, psychotropic medications or suicide. Down the ages, these were not acceptable solutions.

If we look at humanity with a "timeline" view, we see that the ability of righteous people who once withstood the unavoidable vicissitudes of life by adhering to divine law has diminished over the centuries. The endurance, moral strength and strong faith in spiritual values man once obtained is less enjoyed by modern men, women and children who are unable to act in accordance with the same eternal spiritual laws.

In spiritually weak minds, suicide and euthanasia are viable, reasonable means to resolve unendurable poverty, unemployment and personal defeat. It is a grave indication of error in our time when *Final Exit* by British-born Derek Humphrey (founder of The Hemlock Society, 1980) is so famous that it is included in most American library collections and cited whenever euthanasia is challenged in law courts. It has a faithful following of readers and voluntary practitioners of this act. In America, Japan and Sweden—developed countries with a high per capita income, the suicide rate is the highest in the world—fifty-four percent of all deaths were suicides according to UNESCO's data. Highlighting the lack of fulfilment in mere wealth and prestige, forty-four percent of Japanese executives above age 42 suffer some form of mental disorder, according to Japan's Health Ministry. The eminent British psychologist R. D. Laing claimed:

> A child born today in the United Kingdom stands a ten times greater chance of being admitted to a mental hospital than to a University . . . This can be taken as an indication that we are driving our children mad, more effectively than we are genuinely educating them. Perhaps, it is our way of educating them that is driving them mad. (Quoted from Fritjof Capra, *The Turning Point* [New York, 1982], p. 389)

The increased incidence of suicide and chronic depression around the world is strong testimony of profound spiritual

distress and misplaced faith. Though psychotherapy is a popular resource, the observation was made over a century ago that, "Both psychoanalysis and individual psychology fall short. Religious psychology is necessary" (Quoted from Dr. Fritz Kunkel, *In Search of Maturity* [New York, 1943], p. 34). In 1933, Carl Jung wrote:

> The rapid and worldwide growth of a "psychological" interest over the last two decades shows unmistakably that modern man has to some extent turned his attention from material things to his own subjective processes. Should we call this mere curiosity? . . . . This psychological interest of the present time shows that man expects something from psychic life which he has not received from the outer world: something which our religions, doubtless, ought to contain, but no longer do contain—at least for the modern man. The various forms of religion no longer appear to the modern man to come from within—to be expressions of his own psychic life; for him they are to be classed with the things of the outer world. He is vouchsafed no revelation of a spirit that is not of this world; but he tries on a number of religions and convictions as if they were Sunday attire, only to lay them aside again like worn-out clothes. (*Modern Man in Search of a Soul*, pp. 205-6)

John Wesley (1703-1791), the English theologian, evangelist and founder of the Methodist Church, was not one to lay aside his intense spiritual life. His well-placed faith gave him the calm confidence with which he faced the post-Industrial social problems caused by rationalism and materialism and challenged the spiritually degenerated Church of England. His famed Christian missionary zeal was shaped by his longing to bring solace and wisdom to all wretched, uninspired people. When an opportunity arose in 1735 to travel by ship to America

as a missionary, he and his brother went with their mother's abundant blessings. American colonists, however, strongly resisted his rigid enforcement of the moral and ethical codes of the English Church. Embittered and disillusioned, he returned to London after two years, his spiritual zeal weakened.

Mercifully, on his return journey to England, the powerful memory of his experience on the ship towards America arose in his mind to lift his spirit. There had been a severe gale. The other English passengers had panicked and screamed. Remarkably, a small group of Moravian men, women and children on the ship had remained calm and unperturbed. They rivalled the tempestuous winds with sturdy hymns. Their cheerful piety and faith left such a deep impression on his mind that it influenced him all the rest of his days. It was a turning-point in his life. Soon after, he met the Moravian preacher Peter Bohler, who convinced him that a divine flash of illumination alone brings spiritual conviction in life. His faith in God and the preacher's words brought about his great conversion: "I felt my heart strangely warmed. I felt that I did trust in Christ alone for salvation; and an assurance was given me that He had taken my sins, even mine, and saved me from the law of sin and death."

John Henry Newman (1801-1890) is another exemplar of spiritual conviction born of deep faith. A prominent member of the Church of England, he felt compelled to seek a deeper religious life and journeyed to Italy to have discourse with the papal headquarters in Rome. During this time, he endured storms, an earthquake and nearly succumbed fatally to an epidemic in Sicily. A feverish delirium made him painfully aware of the "utter hollowness" of his religious beliefs. They did not provide the inner strength and reliable help he needed in his difficulties and increased his doubts. He felt no relief after recovering slightly. He felt only guilt and remorse. After

a month of convalescence in Italy, his psychological and physical state was still grim.

His meeting with the Vatican priests had been deeply disappointing. It disturbed his mind and worsened his health. Glad to have miraculously survived the epidemic that had killed so many others, he decided to return to England. The ship drifted aimlessly for a week in the windless Strait of Bonifacio. During this misfortune, it dawned in his mind that the same hand of Providence that had struck him down had also lifted him again. The ship's calamity had caused confusion, panic and fear in the crew members and other passengers but he had remained completely indrawn and serene. How is such a desirable attitude of calmness during strife possible? His innately spiritual attitude united with the recent setbacks to make him introspective and contemplative.

He was thirty-two years old when this event gave new meaning and purpose to his life. Opening to the Psalms, he read, "Teach me Thy way, O Lord, and lead me in a plain path" (Psalm 27:11). Profoundly moved by these words, he prayed, "Lead me, O Lord! I need Your help and guidance. I cannot see the way. . . . Lead Kindly Light!" These words soothed his soul and seemed to stir the ocean back to life. A gentle breeze came up suddenly and filled the sails, allowing the ship to resume its journey. Newman noticed none of these external things. His aroused spirit was struggling to express itself. With his thoughts steeped in Divine Grace, he wrote down the words of his beautiful hymn before the ship left the Strait:

> Lead, kindly Light, amid the encircling gloom,
>> Lead thou me on;
> The night is dark, and I am far from home;
>> Lead thou me on.

Keep thou my feet; I do not ask to see
The distant scene; one step enough for me.

I was not ever thus, nor prayed that thou
    Shouldst lead me on;
I loved to choose and see my path; but now
    Lead thou me on.
I loved the garish day, and, spite of fears,
Pride ruled my will: remember not past years.

So long thy power hath blessed me, sure it still
    Will lead me on
O'er moor and fen, o'er crag and torrent, till
    The night is gone,
And with the morn those angel faces smile
Which I have loved long since, and lost awhile.

This hymn, loved by Mahatma Gandhi and sung by countless people around the world, was followed by Newman's fervent *Apologia*, another immortal spiritual classic.

"Of course, the sovereign cure for worry is deep religious faith," said William James. Some scientists verify his view. English biologist Thomas Huxley (1825-1895) once said, "The longer I live, the more obvious it is to me that the most sacred act of a man's life is to say and feel, 'I believe such and such to be true.' All the greatest rewards and all the heaviest penalties of existence cling about that act" (J. Arthur Thomson, *Introduction to Science*, p. 22). His grandson Sir Julian Huxley (1887-1975) said, "The sense of uselessness is the severest shock that any organism can sustain." Our worst apprehensions and fears require our stalwart, unwavering faith in a higher Being.

An eloquent testimony to faith appeared in the *British Medical Journal*:

Nothing in life is more wonderful than faith, the one great moving force which we can neither weigh in the balance nor test in the crucible. Intangible as the ether, ineluctable as gravitation, the radium of the moral and mental spheres, mysterious, indefinable, known only by its effects, faith pours out an unfailing stream of energy while abating nor jot nor tittle of its potency. . . . Faith is indeed one of the miracles of human life which science is as ready to accept as it is to study its effects. (British Medical Journal, June 18, 1910 issue. Quoted in *The Power of Prayer*, ed. Rt. Rev. Patterson, p. 179. Quoted from *Religion as a Quest for Values*, p. 26)

There is ample evidence of the "therapy of faith," a quiet self-surrender to the divine recuperative power. We commonly think of it as "placing myself in the hands of God." Serene faith in God and our identity with the universal, creative divine vitality that operates within and without, heals us. Along with faith, we must cultivate the other spiritual principles.

Faith in God brings patience and forbearance. By seeking God in every breath and through constant prayer, Gandhiji's purity and faith in God proved his triumph over worldliness. His utter reliance on God to "lead kindly on" his soul strengthened his mind and resolve. Though the work at hand always received his intense concentration and appeared to take priority, he always withdrew himself for daily periods of prayer and contemplation. He did not allow any duty or difficulty to obliterate his spiritual life. The great Avataras, saints and sages have all testified that the power of thought guided them to experience their own divinity while living in the world.

"Nature, time and patience are the three great physicians," says an Irish proverb. Though desire for freedom impels both spiritual and secular principles of faith, they differ vastly.

Occasionally, they intercept, as in the practical spiritual principle that a disciplined spiritual life includes practical, healthy values about our diet.

*(7) Correct dietary guidelines.* A healthy diet seasoned with impure thoughts does not produce the desired effect; a healthy diet accompanied by pure thoughts has the desired effect. Swami Vivekananda says:

> We must remember that, according to the Sankhya philosophy, the *Sattva, Rajas* and *Tamas,* which in the state of homogenous equilibrium form the *Prakriti,* and in the heterogeneous disturbed condition form the universe—are both the substance and the quality of *Prakriti.* As such, they are the materials out of which every human form has been manufactured, and the predominance of the *sattva* material is what is absolutely necessary for spiritual development. (*C. W.,* III: 66)

"When the food (*ahara*) is pure, the *sattva* element gets purified and the memory becomes unwavering" (*Chan. Up.,* 7. 26. 2). Sri Ramakrishna says, "*Sattva* preserves, *rajas* creates, and *tamas* destroys" (*Gospel,* p. 267). Swami Vivekananda says:

> Certain regulations as to food are necessary; we must use that food which brings us the purest mind. If you go into a menagerie, you will find this demonstrated at once. You see the elephants, huge animals, but calm and gentle; and if you go towards the cages of the lions and tigers, you find them restless, showing how much difference has been made by food. (*C. W.,* I: 136)

It is very easy to take care about material food, but mental work must go along with it; then gradually our spiritual self will become stronger and stronger, and the physical self less assertive. Then will food hurt you no more. The great danger is that every man wants to jump at the highest ideal, but jumping is not the way. That ends only in a fall. We are bound down here, and we have to break our chains slowly. This is called *Viveka*, discrimination. (*C. W.*, IV: 7)

After reviewing various biased opinions about food and what the *Shastras* have to say about it, Swami Vivekananda introduced the broad-minded view of Hinduism:

All these contentions have no end; they are going on unceasingly. Now the judicious view admitted by all in regard to this vexed question is to take such food as is substantial and nutritious and, at the same time, easily digested. The food should be such as contains the greatest nutriment in the smallest compass, and be at the same time quickly assimilable [sic]; otherwise, it has necessarily to be taken in large quantity, and consequently the whole day is required only to digest it. If all the energy is spent only in digesting food, what will there be left to do other works? (*C. W.*, V: 486)

In *Bhakti-Yoga* Swamiji gives a helpful hint to beginners:

But the control of the grosser is absolutely necessary to enable one to arrive at the control of the finer. The beginner, therefore, must pay particular attention to all such dietetic rules as have come down from the line of his accredited teachers . . . So it stands to reason that discrimination in the choice of food is necessary for the attainment of this higher state of mental composition which cannot be easily obtained otherwise. (*C. W.*, III: 66)

A clear definition and orientation to spiritual fulfilment fixes life's priorities. Mind takes the right direction when we strive cheerfully with self-control for the spiritual goal while living in the world.

*(8) Correct use of Prana.* We have understood many things but we do not know or care to know what life is and where it comes from. The entire creation emerges and is sustained by *Prana*, the essential life force that pervades all life. Swami Vivekananda says:

> It is the Prana that is manifesting as motion; it is the Prana that is manifesting as gravitation, as magnetism. It is the Prana that is manifesting as the actions of the body, as the nerve currents, as thought force. . . .
>
> How to control the Prana is the one idea of Pranayama. All the trainings and exercises in this regard are for that one end. Each man must begin where he stands, must learn how to control the things that are nearest to him. This body is very near to us, nearer than anything in the external universe, and this mind is the nearest of all. The Prana which is working this mind and body is the nearest to us of all the Prana in this universe. This little wave of the Prana which represents our own energies, mental and physical, is the nearest to us of all the waves of the infinite ocean of Prana. If we can succeed in controlling that little wave, then alone we can hope to control the whole of Prana. (*C. W.*, I: 147-9)
>
> By Prana are meant the nervous forces governing and moving the whole body, which also manifest themselves as thought. (*C. W.*, II: 454)
>
> This Prana is electricity, it is magnetism; it is thrown out by the brain as thought. (*C. W.*, II: 30)

Nothing affects this essential element of life. Through its energy, we live, breathe, think and move. Patanjali says that we can control the *Prana* by controlling the breath through *Pranayama* (*Yoga Sutras*, I: 34). Swamiji says, "you simply throw the air out, and draw it in, and hold it for some time, that is all, and by that, the mind will become a little calmer" (*C. W.*, I: 223).

Tragically, we waste a tremendous amount of *Prana* when we dwell on thoughts pleasing to the senses, mull over our memories, and retell our personal history. Indulgence strengthens desire. Because desire is never wholly satisfied, we feel oppressed. Swamiji says, "Thought is the finest expression of *Prana* available to human beings." *Pranayama* verily means the control of thought. We arouse and strengthen *Prana* through spiritual thoughts and practices. Focusing on the breath, for example, calms and concentrates the mind. Whenever the mind wanders in meditation, gently bringing our attention back to the breath renews our concentration on the object of our meditation. This method teaches us to control the most turbulent thoughts and experience the extraordinary, innate peaceful nature of the mind.

Using a light switch, we efficiently control light and darkness in a room. The mantra turns off the mind's "sensory switch of ignorance" and helps us use the vital energy of *Prana* in a wise and selfless way. We cannot neglect the mind's power to utilize its inexhaustible energy for self-control, happiness, purity and peace that bring contentment to the mind. Swamiji says:

> The mind has to be gradually and systematically brought under control. The will has to be strengthened by slow, continuous and persevering drill. This is no child's play, no fad to be tried one day and discarded the next. It

is a life's work; and the end to be attained is well worth all that it can cost us to reach it; being nothing less than the realisation of our absolute oneness with the Divine. Surely, with this end in view, and with the knowledge that we can certainly succeed, no price can be too great to pay. (*C. W.*, V: 294)

"The impure mind is that mind which is polluted by the world and the pure mind is free from it" (*Pancadasi*, X. 116). The pure, spiritually enlightened mind is filled with bliss.

*(9) Correct value of cheerfulness.* "A merry heart maketh a cheerful countenance, but by sorrow of the heart the spirit is broken" (Proverbs, 15: 13). Lasting happiness comes to a spiritually enlightened mind with faith in the spiritual goal. Ordinary happiness, fleeting and superficial, comes from evanescent material objects and events.

A cheerless existence is a sign of weakness in the mind and body, which are interdependent. Swamiji says:

> The weak have no place here, in this life or in any other life. Weakness leads to slavery. Weakness leads to all kinds of misery, physical and mental. Weakness is death. There are hundreds of thousands of microbes surrounding us, but they cannot harm us unless we become weak, until the body is ready and predisposed to receive them. There may be a million microbes of misery, floating about us. Never mind! They dare not approach us, they have no power to get a hold on us, until the mind is weakened. This is the great fact. . . . He who falters at first will get stronger and stronger, and the voice [of strength] will increase in volume until the truth takes possession of our hearts, and courses through our veins, and permeates our bodies. (*C. W.*, II: 3, 202)

Freud believed that humour indicates maturity. According to Fritjof Capra, "Health is really a multidimensional phenomenon involving interdependent physical, psychological and social aspects . . . Physical disease may be balanced by a positive mental attitude and social support, so that the overall state is one of well-being" (Fritjof Capra, *The Turning Point* [London: Flamingo Ed., 1982], p. 355). Cheerfulness transforms a cell's metabolism by improving the production of neurochemical and endocrine hormones, which reinforce the body's immune system.

The poet W. H. Auden claimed that we are considered successful when we value work, worship, and "carnival" or happy celebration. Cheerfulness has been introduced to the medical profession with good results. Drs. Carl and Stephanie Simonton make humour and laughter a significant part of psychotherapy and medical treatment for recovering cancer patients. At UCLA's Neuropsychiatric Institute and Hospital in California, a depressed, spiritually broken cancer patient confined to a wheelchair improved considerably after six months of integrated therapy that stimulated his cheerfulness (*Time*, Mar. 12, 1990).

We generally feel that dying is complex and mysterious. The dying often lose communication with relatives and friends who are reluctant or unable for various reasons to remain by their side. Humour and laughter are confirmed palliatives to many patients as they face death and good therapy for their caregivers. The essentials of living alleviate the difficulties of dying. The social value of communication and solidarity that this soothing "medicine" provides far outweighs the discomfort expressed by medical providers in the *Journal of the American Medical Association*: "We blame our uneasiness on many things—dealing with death, fatigue, malpractice threats. Thus, we can easily excuse ourselves for leaving no time for laughter"

(*JAMA*, December 21, 1979, p. 2765). Medieval doctors measured the relative proportions of four basic humours to determine a person's well-being. It may be helpful for caretakers of the sick and dying to remember that "humor" derives from the Latin *humor* or "moisture" (pl., *humores*).

Vast funds pour into psychobiological research and advanced biofeedback techniques by prestigious medical schools and yield positive results: cheerfulness effectively alters harmful inner thoughts that lead to depression, fear, and anxiety. The financial power of scientific research, however, cannot approach the spiritual power of the Indwelling God whose lasting cure is a happy and peaceful mind centred on God.

The moral value of cheerfulness adds a beneficial dimension to spiritual power as we think of God with faith and devotion in life's struggle. Awed by Mahatma Gandhi's self-discipline and courteous humour, his bitterest opponents respected him. This encouraged him and advanced his influence on matters of grave consequence. When a friend asked him, "Is humour necessary for life?" he replied, "If there were no humour, I would have committed suicide long ago!" (*Know Gandhi in One Hundred Ways*, p. 26).

Humour reflects the infinite wealth of joy that we sometimes feel. Its creative expression is so diverse. Humour can be jolly, dry, witty and even morose, depending on the experience of the humorist. It can be sophisticated or provincial. When Abraham Lincoln's grave burden of responsibility to the young American nation got the upper hand, he relied on his own rustic humour to lift his drooping spirit. His talent for mimicry, great store of hilarious anecdotes and willingness to make himself the object of his jokes bridged the gap between himself and many an adversary.

Sir Thomas More (1478-1535), the bold English statesman and author of *Utopia* who is considered a saint by many, expressed humour even as he drew his last breath. He seemed to have transcended his fear of death before he mounted the scaffold for his beheading at the command of King Henry VIII. Moments before his execution, he joked with the executioner about his neck being too short for the axe—the executioner's honour might be at stake, he quipped. He then pulled his beard away from the execution block and joked that because it had never offended his King, it should not come under the axe.

Nobel Laureate Albert Schweitzer (1875-1965) maintained a formidable work schedule and creativity way into his nineties. "Laughter is said to remove the rust from the mind, lubricate our inner machinery, and enable us to do our work. The more you laugh, the healthier you become. If you make others laugh, it is equivalent to doing social service." Albert Schweitzer consciously added a strong dose of humour to his driving sense of moral purpose and creativity to benefit all. All three, he maintained, made his body a bad host for any disease, which always quickly left it. He used his propensity for wry wit in a conscious effort to help others too. When his staff came together at dinnertime, the most welcomed course was his amusing anecdote or witty remark. His "humour therapy" worked wonders on the exhausted doctors and nurses. It is interesting to note that today, some hospitals provide laughing rooms where patients can watch comedies and read cartoons. A gifted pianist, the venerable Schweitzer would also play hymns composed by Johann Sebastian Bach on two old, battered pianos—one in the staff dining hall and the other in the privacy of his bungalow—to release the pressures and tensions of the hospital work. He was well aware of the prophylactic effect of music and mirth to keep chemical balance in the brain. It has been said, "His story is a living sermon on the brotherhood of man."

For the great writer Lin Yutang, laughter represented "the chemical function of humor: to change the character of our thought." Norman Cousins wrote:

> Science and common sense converge in the ultimate mission of human intelligence—the full potentiation [sic] of the individual. This process is not confined to the development of human abilities. It involves in equal measure the way human beings ward off breakdown and cope with it when it occurs. It has to do with the will to live and the physiological benefits of creativity and the positive emotions. It assigns a proper value to hope, faith, laughter, and confidence in the life force. (*Human Options*, p. 206)

There is an essential distinction between "fun" and "joy." Fun is contagious and tends to lead us away from morality and virtue. The joy of spirituality, as we know from the lives of the great saints and sages, is an influence that spreads rapidly with a transforming, regenerating, global effect. "Fun" has become the single, most important value in modern society in the West. The subconscious impact of this value inundates the media and begins shaping citizens from childhood to think that through fun they will be happy, acquire learning more easily, be creative and live long. They must have fun with family, fun with friends, fun with pets, fun at school, fun at work and even fun at the temple or church. The element of fun drives governments, education and virtually every industry. People are conditioned to seek and expect fun in their personal, community and social life. One commentator remarked during a lecture at the Indian Institute of Management at Kolkata's Centre for Human Values:

> ... A humorless teacher has much less chance of success now in the field of higher education, especially in the

Humanities and Social Sciences, than a humorous one. A joke or two is routinely planned even by a popular science lecturer. The omnipresence of jokes and funny remarks in mass media has spilled over to the atmosphere of the classroom. Education has to be fun.

Similarly, big companies urge their managers to take "structured fun" courses. For more than a decade now, professional stand-up comedians are regularly hired by big offices to entertain and train their personnel, to relax them and to teach them how to relax and befriend clients. Thus, fun has become a marketing mantra. (*Global Vedanta*, Winter 2003-04, Vol. IX, No. 1, p. 8-9)

We must conclude that although appreciation of humour may help us to achieve success in worldly life, fun or humour do not provide us with the lasting joy of a self-controlled, contented mind derived from a spiritual orientation in life.

## TRANSFORMING EFFECT OF SPIRITUAL THOUGHTS
### *THE PLACEBO EFFECT*

Modern science provides ample proof of the effect of thoughts on the body. In *Timeless Healing*, Dr. Herbert Benson writes, "Most of the history of medicine is the history of the placebo effect." Placebos are inert or innocuous substances. They replace the active ingredient of a medicine when researchers test the efficacy of the actual medicine in a controlled experiment. Half of the participants take the actual medicine; the other half takes the placebo. Participants do not know which they have taken; also, they may or may not be told about the existence of the placebo in the experiment. However, they are told that the drug is effective.

For example, patients suffering from arthritis (a disease often attributed to emotional stress) report the remission of crippling physical symptoms or complete removal of pain when taking placebos of various analgesics (or substances like chondroitin sulfate or MSM, both well-known vitamin supplements) in controlled clinical trials. Some decades ago, an experiment with a placebo on 300 patients suffering various dysfunctions, toothaches, headaches and the like, was conducted by the Boston Dispensary. Many of the patients receiving the placebo of an empty syringe in place of one filled with medicine were temporarily relieved of their symptoms, some of them permanently.

Some patients, whose breast cancer metastasized into various parts of the body, report that their tumours diminished in size or completely disappeared over time. There is no definitive credit given to the placebo effect in these cases, since there is a broad range of survival time in these cases, stretched over weeks or years. Still, the effect of a placebo in the form of pills or some other element must be taken into account, along with other legitimate factors in the cure of fatal diseases.

One of the most significant elements in the cure of disease is the beneficial relationship of the doctor to the patient. Norman Cousins writes:

> The practice of medicine, as has been emphasized over the centuries by almost every great medical teacher (from Hippocrates to Holmes, from Galen to Cannon, from Castiglione to Osler), calls first of all for a deeply human response by the physician to the cry of the patient for help . . . The physician who understands the importance of sitting

at the bedside, even though his presence may actually be in the nature of a placebo equivalent, is attending to a prevalent and quintessential need. . . . [it is] the overriding issue before medicine today. (Norman Cousins, *Human Options* [New York, 1981], p. 214)

Research shows that placebos bring about mental relief as well as occasional relief of the disorder in the unsuspecting patient. Prayers, declarations of hope and encouraging words are themselves healing placebos when we express them to someone who is ill or grieving and who may or may not be aware of them.

In every stage of life, love is a catalyst to recovery and has a great role to play. The most potent medicine given by a doctor with a poor attitude cannot cure anyone; a simple sugar pill given with love and compassion works wonders. Citing Hippocrates, "A patient who is mortally sick might yet recover from belief in the goodness of his physician," Dr. Deepak Chopra confirms, "Numerous studies have corroborated this, by showing that people who trust their doctor and surrender themselves to his care are likelier to recover than those who approach medicine with distrust, fear, and antagonism" (*Quantum Healing*, pp. 30-1).

Doctors are expected to treat their patients with sympathy and with the promise of helping them to outgrow their limitations and achieve their full glory as human beings. If doctors treat them with a good deal of care, love and affection, patients will respond quickly. We consider the following remark by Goethe to be the finest maxim of any form of psychotherapy: "If we take people as they are, we make them worse. If we treat them as if they were what they ought to be, we help them to become what they are capable of becoming" (Quoted from *The Doctor and the Soul*, p. 96).

The world's illness and pain should stimulate compassion and humility in us and reverence for God, the Indweller in all.

Whether the unhealthy condition is a physical, psychological or emotional one, it originates in the mind; the mind dwelling on the subject of pain and illness constantly renews those objective perceptions in the mind and conveys them to the body, which experiences them through the senses. Most of this goes on unconsciously in the mind. We seldom realize that we can improve and even reverse our negative condition by constantly thinking positive thoughts and constantly rejecting negative ones. Swami Vivekananda says:

> And here is the test of truth—anything that makes you weak physically, intellectually, and spiritually, reject as poison; there is no life in it, it cannot be true. Truth is strengthening. Truth is purity, truth is all-knowledge; truth must be strengthening, must be enlightening, must be invigorating. (*C. W.*, III: 224-5)

Most people believe that swallowing a pill is more tangible—even if it is inert—and therefore more promising of a cure, than the ideas and suggestions of well-being and immortality that nurture the spiritual way of life. We will need the placebo as long as we continue to identify with the body and remain ignorant of ourselves as divine, eternal beings. The power of the "placebo" of spiritual thoughts *consciously* brings about miraculous reversals in human thought and behaviour. Statements that defy even life-threatening illnesses, such as, "I am definitely going to recover," or, "I do not identify at all with this cancer; I know I am much more than this tumour; inside, it really does not touch me at all," use the powerful inner healing capacity of the patients' reasoning faculty.

## *THE NOCEBO EFFECT*

Researchers quickly applied the inversion of the placebo in their controlled test studies. Where the placebo is a fake drug, the "nocebo" uses a real medication with the suggestion given by the doctor to the patient that the drug does *not* work. Although the drug is viable, the patient does not feel better because of the doctor's signal. The nocebo effect has a negative influence on the body and the psyche, and opposes the positive influence of the placebo, according to the findings of Dr. Benson and his colleagues, Julie Corliss and Geoffrey Crowley. We all know the effects of simple repetitions on the minds of developing children. Eventually they personify what they hear repeatedly from family members, teachers, etc. "You are such a bad child!" "Stupid child, you are so ignorant!" "Stop bothering me with questions!" "You'll never learn!" The statements drummed into their ears are certain to produce dull, criminal, timid, unmotivated and unconfident future adults, susceptible to any suggestion that presents itself. A story cited by Swami Abhedananda illustrates the effects of a negative external thought-suggestion:

> An experiment was made upon a healthy young man who was going to his office in the morning. Six of his friends put their heads together to give a suggestion to his mind, without letting him know that they were doing it. As he started out of his home, one of his friends, who was standing at the street corner, looked at him and said, "How do you do? You look very sick; what is the matter with you? How strange you look today! Are you sick?" The young man replied, "No, I am very well; I have no trouble with me. I am all right." . . . Thus, six friends held him up at different stations on his way to the office and they all said the same thing. Then it got on his nerves. The young

man went to his office and said to himself: "I do not feel very well now. What is the matter with me? All my friends say I am sick; I must be sick." After a few hours, he began to feel the effect and was convinced that he was sick with a high fever. He stayed in bed and called in a doctor. The doctor came, but the man suffered for a time from the effect of these suggestions. The next day, it was explained to him that it was all a joke. (Swami Abhedananda, *Science of Psychic Phenomena* [Calcutta: Ramakrishna Vedanta Math, 1966])

The spiritually motivated will to improve one's situation has great power on a vacillating, fearful mind to make it contend with the necessities of life in a concentrated way. This may be temporary or lasting depending on our individual capacity to improve our quality of life. Our capacity increases immeasurably when we combine it with prayer, faith, resoluteness and dedication to higher and nobler ideals.

## GUIDING FORCE OF DYNAMIC SPIRITUAL THOUGHT

Spiritual thought has powerful individual and universal consequences. Two incidents during Swamiji's itinerant life illustrate this fact. Swamiji relates the first:

I was once travelling in the Himalayas, and the long road stretched before us. We poor monks cannot get any one to carry us, so we had to make all the way on foot. There was an old man with us. The way goes up and down for hundreds of miles, and when that old monk saw what was before him, he said, "Oh, sir, how to cross it; I cannot walk any more, my chest will break." I said to him, "Look down at your feet." He did so, and I said, "The road that is under your feet is the road that you have passed over and is the same road that you see before you; it will soon be under your feet." The highest things . . . are under your feet. You can swallow the stars by the handful if you want; such is your real nature. Be strong, get beyond all superstitions, and be free. (*C. W.*, VIII: 186-7)

One of Swamiji's disciples described the second incident:

One morning after visiting the temple of Mother Durga, the Swami was passing through a place where there were a large tank of water on one side and a high wall on the other. Here he was surrounded by a large troop of wild monkeys. They were not willing to allow him to pass along that way. They howled and shrieked and clutched at his feet as he strode. As they pressed closer, he began to run; but the faster he ran, the faster came the monkeys, and they began to bite at him. When it seemed impossible for him to escape, he heard an old sannyasi calling out to him: "Face the brutes." The words brought him to his senses. He turned and boldly faced the irate monkeys. As soon as he did that, they fell back and fled. With reverence and gratitude, he gave the traditional greeting to the sannyasi, who smilingly responded with the same, and walked away. In a New York lecture years later, the Swami referred to this incident and pointed to its moral: "That is a lesson for all life—face the terrible, face it boldly. Like the monkeys, the hardships of life fall back when we cease to flee before them. If we are ever to gain freedom, it must be by conquering nature, never by running away. Cowards never win victories. We have to fight fear and troubles and ignorance if we expect them to flee before us." (*The Life of Swami Vivekananda by His Eastern and Western Disciples* [Calcutta, 1979], p. 214)

Swami Vivekananda was fearless and heroic in temperament. In contrast, Holy Mother lived a simple, rustic life. That is the outer aspect of her personality for a common person. However, she was wholly Divine, although she was living the most ordinary life. Once, Holy Mother discovered that she was being followed:

> On another occasion, at Jayrambati, she was pursued by a cranky man. She ran around a haystack several times. Then it occurred to her, "Why am I running? Am I not Shakti Herself? She turned round, threw the man on the ground, and putting her knee on the chest of the man gave him such slaps that his crankiness was cured at least for the time being. (Swami Tapasyananda, *Sri Sarada Devi, The Holy Mother*, pp. 96-7)

The cranky man was Harish, a young married devotee of the Master. Fortunately for Harish, he came to live for some time with Sri Ramakrishna at Dakshineswar and developed a strong spiritual thirst. Sri Ramakrishna admired his spiritual zeal. He loved and praised him very much during this period. Unfortunately, his wife felt unduly threatened by his long absence from home and by his intense spiritual desire. Without Harish's knowledge, she plied him with drugs and charms to counteract his spiritual tendency for renunciation. Harish's mind had become deranged due to the influence of these drugs when he went to see Holy Mother at Kamarpukur, near Jayrambati. Holy Mother's punishment had a permanent effect; when Harish later went to Vrindaban, he became completely normal after some time.

The power of thought guides us to experience our own divinity; we are in truth Radiant Immortal Atman. Our thoughts may be compared to ocean waves, and the Atman or Self to the ocean in which waves subside. The most unique cultivation of spirituality in the mind occurs when we project loving thoughts to the world. Swamiji says, "Every good thought that we send to the world without thinking of any return, will be stored up there and break one link in the chain, and make us purer and purer, until we become the purest of mortals" (*C. W.*, I: 116).

We must cultivate pure thoughts unceasingly in the mind with faith in our just reward: ignorance of our spiritual nature is replaced by knowledge of the Self. The holy thought-vibrations of all the avatars, saints and sages exist in the realm of thought. They are eternal. Swamiji says, "The purity of these few *Paramahamsas* [monks of the highest order] is all that holds the world together. If they should all die out and leave it, the world would go to pieces. They do good by simply being, and they know it not; they just are . . ." (*C. W.*, VII: 85). Thinking of the events of their lives and their teachings attunes our consciousness to theirs, attracting their thoughts to our mind. Swamiji says:

> The highest men are calm, silent, and unknown. They are the men who really know the power of thought; they are sure that, even if they go into a cave and close the door and simply think five true thoughts and then pass away, these five thoughts of theirs will live through eternity. Indeed such thoughts will penetrate through the mountains, cross the oceans, and travel through the world. They will enter deep into human hearts and brains and raise up men and women who will give them practical expression in the workings of human life. (*C. W.*, I: 106)

Millions of exemplary lives were transformed by the eternal dynamic spiritual thoughts generated by great prophets who convey and embody Vedanta, a system of living thought and personal conduct. This attunement of mind to a higher ideal

15

closely relates to the concept of service, according to Swami Vivekananda. To achieve the higher ideal (the effect) we must focus on the means (the cause) to achieve that ideal. In his lecture, "Work and Its Secret," Swami Vivekananda says:

> One of the greatest lessons I have learnt in my life is to pay as much attention to the means of work as to its end . . . Once the ideal is chosen, and the means determined, we may almost let go the ideal, because we are sure it will be there, when the means are perfected. When the cause is there, there is no more difficulty about the effect, the effect is bound to come. If we take care of the cause, the effect will take care of itself. . . . The means are the cause: attention to the means, therefore, is the great secret of life. We also read this in the *Gita* and learn that we have to work, constantly work with all our power; to put our whole mind in the work, whatever it be, that we are doing. At the same time, we must not be attached. That is to say, we must not be drawn away from the work by anything else; still, we must be able to quit the work whenever we like. (*C. W.*, II: 1-2)

Therefore, Swamiji also emphatically explains the means:

> There is a great tendency in modern times to talk too much of work and decry thought. Doing is very good, but that comes from thinking. Little manifestations of energy through the muscles are called work. But where there is no thought, there will be no work. Fill the brain, therefore, with high thoughts, highest ideals, place them day and night before you, and out of that will come great work. Talk not about impurity, but say that we are pure. We have hypnotised ourselves into this thought that we are little, that we are born, and that we are going to die, and into a constant state of fear. . . .

Men are taught from childhood that they are weak and sinners. Teach them that they are all glorious children of immortality, even those who are the weakest in manifestation. Let positive, strong, helpful thought enter into their brains from very childhood. Lay yourselves open to these thoughts, and not to weakening and paralysing ones. Say to your own minds, "I am He, I am He." Let it ring day and night in your minds like a song, and at the point of death declare, "I am He." That is the Truth; the infinite strength of the world is yours. Drive out the superstition that has covered your minds. Let us be brave. Know the Truth and practise the Truth. The goal may be distant, but awake, arise, and stop not till the goal is reached. (*C. W.*, II: 85-7 passim)

## HOW TO BECOME PEACEFUL: A BRIEF STATEMENT

At the very least, we can prevent the build-up of unspiritual impulses and desires by simply leaving the place where hostility, annoyance, or corruption appears. That will certainly help us to become more peaceful. However, this gives us temporary, not lasting benefit. On the other hand, faith in God and conviction of the higher meaning of life, supported by correct values are essential for spiritual progress. All the practical, correct spiritual principles of thought and activity point to the power within the mind to make it peaceful. The serene mind, that makes the entire organism peaceful, submissive and in harmony with the Divine will, alone alleviates stress. The inspiring descriptions of the transforming power of spiritual thought may serve to enlighten and encourage us. Cultivating our attunement to the eternal thought-vibrations of the Holy Ones, we will purify our mind and fill it with the highest ideals.

In one of his inspired talks, Swamiji taught his pupils, "Mind is an instrument in the hand of Atman, just as body is an instrument in the hand of mind. Matter is motion outside, mind is motion inside" (*C. W.*, VII: 95-6). Mind is the instrument of thought, which moves it. Spiritual thought, knowledge of the Self, is the greatest motive force for individual and common welfare.

# CONCLUSION

## THE DEEPER SIGNIFICANCE OF SPIRITUAL LIFE

*In man, the things which are not measurable are more important than those which are measurable.*

Dr. Alexis Carrel,
*Man, The Unknown*

## SOME SIGNIFICANT COMMENTARIES

According to the neurophysiologist and Nobelist Sir John Eccles, the scientific community is partially accountable for man's moral and existential dilemma. We do not think of the spiritual treasure we possess; we have been convinced that we should think instead of our imagined deficiency. In his Gifford Lectures at the University of Edinburgh (1978-1979), he said:

Man has lost his way ideologically in this age. It is what has been called the predicament of mankind. I think that science has gone too far in breaking down man's belief in his spiritual greatness . . . and has given him the belief that he is merely an insignificant animal that has arisen by chance and necessity in an insignificant planet lost in the great cosmic immensity. (John C. Eccles, *The Human Psyche* [New York Heidelberg Berlin: Springer-Verlag, 1980], p. 251)

Thoughtful persons scrutinize narrow or restricted views, seeking a broader dimension and application based on truth. Materialism in any age cannot provide us with healthy spiritual values that give us purpose and meaning, and that help us realize the limitless immensity of the soul. Liberalism and humanitarianism also fall short of the noble goal of human life. Any idealism that ignores Self-awareness is an incomplete idealism founded on a false ideal. The neglected spiritual heart of man has become a house of cards that flutters apart at the least disturbance, leaving us without refuge. In *Modern Man in Search of a Soul*, Carl Jung observes:

> The modern man has lost all the metaphysical certainties of his medieval brother, and set up in their place the ideals of material security, general welfare and humaneness. But it takes more than an ordinary dose of optimism to make it appear that these ideals are still unshaken. . . . Science has destroyed even the refuge of the inner life. What was once a sheltering haven has become a place of terror. (*Modern Man in Search of a Soul*, pp. 204-5)

As a result, modern man feels isolated, alone and abandoned and broods constantly on his material and physical needs.

According to J. Bradley Hoskisson, in his book, *Loneliness: An Explanation, A Cure* (London, [S. I.] Thorsons, 1963), "Loneliness is the conscious experience of separation from something or someone." It is partly a matter of seeking attention from others, since our attention is fixed on ourselves and on our feeling of self-pity. It is not the same as solitariness. Man is solitary by choice, has strength of mind, and depends on inner, soul awareness; man is lonely by indifference and neglect, has weakness of mind, and depends on external, impermanent material things.

Jung understood the deeper significance of certain facts of modern life:

I should like to call attention to the following facts. During the past thirty years, people from all the civilized countries of the earth have consulted me. I have treated many hundreds of patients, the larger number being Protestants, a smaller number of Jews, and not more than five or six believing Catholics. Among all my patients in the second half of life—that is to say over thirty-five—there has not been one whose problem in the last resort was not that of finding a religious outlook on life. It is safe to say that every one of them fell ill because he had lost that which the living religions of every age have given to their followers and none of them has been really healed who did not regain his religious outlook. This of course has nothing whatever to do with a particular creed or membership of a church. (Jung, *The Collected Works*, Vol. XI [1958], p. 334)

Man is never helped in his suffering by what he thinks for himself, but only by revelations of a wisdom greater than his own. It is this which lifts him out of his distress. (*Modern Man in Search of a Soul*, pp. 240-1)

The wisdom Jung speaks of is spiritual and eternal culture. Swami Vivekananda says:

It is a change of the soul itself for the better that alone will cure the evils of life. No amount of force, or government, or legislative cruelty will change the conditions of a race, but it is spiritual culture and ethical culture alone that can change wrong racial tendencies for the better. Thus these races of the West are eager for some new thought, for some new philosophy; the religion they have had, Christianity, although good and glorious in many respects, has been imperfectly understood, and is, as understood hitherto, found to be insufficient. The thoughtful men of the West find in our ancient philosophy, especially in the Vedanta, the new impulse of thought they are seeking, the very spiritual food and drink for which they are hungering and thirsting. And it is no wonder that this is so. (*C. W.*, III: 182)

Dr. Carrel stressed the importance of gathering the mind and unifying the desires through prayerful meditation. He regarded these as the moral and spiritual remedies for the consequences of the emotions:

> Physiological activities must remain outside the field of consciousness. They are disturbed when we turn our attention towards them. Thus psychoanalysis, in directing the mind of the patient upon himself, may aggravate his state of unbalance. Instead of indulging in self-analysis it is better to escape from oneself through an effort that does not scatter the mind. (*Man the Unknown*, p. 140)

## KEY TO HAPPINESS AND MENTAL STABILITY

Obedience to the universal laws of enlightenment and peaceful living is the key to a collected mind and happiness. On the other hand, obedience to the dictates of a sensate culture is the gaping door to the inherent defects of instinctive living: nervousness, constant tension, discontent, conflict, war and terrorism. These are the inevitable results of an acquisitive society with the basic cultural values of competition, prosperity, hedonism and global power. If we allow ourselves to be trapped and deluded by stubborn dedication to sensate culture, we deprive ourselves of spiritual harmony, enlightenment and unity.

Are we perfectly free from anxiety? Are we satisfied in the Self, without the need of external things to make us happy? Are we capable of dwelling in the awareness of Pure Consciousness or Reality? Are we unshaken by the heaviest sorrow? The teachings of the *Bhagavad Gita* (VI: 20-23) answers these questions in the affirmative. It is the promise of God to man that we are capable of these when we are established in the Self. The great wisdom teachers of humanity all attained this inner stability through knowledge of the Self. They came to teach us that unless we achieve this inner stability, we will be broken from within, as well as from without, by trying circumstances. Inner stability protects us from inner and outer destruction when adversity comes to us. It makes our lives meaningful, healthy and creative. It purifies the mind, which can then enjoy a taste of eternal bliss.

Yet, "Human beings have been able to comprehend everything in the world except their uniqueness" (Norman Cousins, *Human Options*, p. 206). The kingdom of God is within us. The less we depend on external things for our happiness, the more we enjoy the blessings of spiritual life. This is the supremely important message of eminent, moral men and women who have embraced the spiritual life. According to Bertrand Russell, "These sincere believers are valuable to the world because they keep alive the conviction that life of the spirit is what is of the most importance to men and women." He expressed his profound appreciation for the great religious world teachers: "What is of most value in human life is more analogous to what all the great religious teachers have spoken of. If they were to die, most of what is best would vanish out of life."

A disciplined spiritual life combats the weakness of negative thoughts. It strengthens us in adversity by giving us forbearance. This and other spiritual values make our recovery from hardship a lasting one and help us prevent certain difficulties and sorrows that devastate others who lack spiritual consciousness.

We cannot begin to measure the value of the transforming power of positive spiritual thoughts as we make every effort towards Self-Realization. They bring stability to the mind, which can then confront and resolve every adversity in life through clear thinking and righteous actions. The real remedy for human suffering and alienation is the knowledge of the Self that removes weakness and restores us to an integrated state of well-being.

## EXCHANGING EGOISM FOR IDEALISM

Wordsworth wrote, "Unless above himself he erects himself, how poor a thing is man." Intellectual growth and material success unaccompanied by higher, noble qualities only make us egoistic, aggressive, and victimized by our faults. We must free ourselves by eschewing egocentric life. "A too powerful ego is a prison from which a man must escape if he is to enjoy the world to the full. A capacity for genuine affection is one of the marks of the man who has escaped from this prison of self," said Bertrand Russell (*The Conquest of Happiness*, p. 185). Spiritual values stabilize, encourage and support society. They alone make us truly peaceful, self-confident and fearless.

We must exchange our belief in the strong ego for the conviction of a mighty ideal: "This is the true joy of life—in being used for a purpose recognized by yourself as a mighty one," said George Bernard Shaw. "Political action, social work, this "*ism*," that "*ology*," are all incomplete, futile actions unless accompanied by a new and elevated mode of awareness. In other words, the true revolution is revelation," editor John

White writes in the introduction of *The Highest State of Consciousness* (p. ix).

## SPIRITUAL DEFINITION OF HEALTH

The World Health Organization defines health from a secular point of view that only suggests that we are more than a complex psychophysical organism: "Health is the state of complete physical, mental and social well-being and does not consist merely in the absence of disease and deficiency." The Hindu scriptures go further and remove any doubt. They declare that the essence of our being is spiritual—our real nature of overall well-being, or the fullness of health, has an awakened spiritual foundation. The *sine qua non* of spiritual awakening is moral goodness.

Spiritual living alone, not drugs and vaccines, give us lasting protection from disease and sorrow. We must abandon our materialism and embrace a spiritual attitude. Swamiji says, "How to transcend the senses without disturbing health is what we want to learn" (*C. W.*, VI: 129). Every sincere spiritual aspirant must accept the fact that spiritual unfoldment alone eliminates enmity and stress. The secret of a peaceful state of mind is the proper valuation of life and intense spiritual practice in the form of meditation, worship and dedicated service to humanity. We must become convinced that it is worthier to change our outlook on life than to change our environment or secular status. Our conscious change of attitude carried out in our daily activities will give us ethical and spiritual satisfaction as well as a healthy state of mind.

Many also equate health with physical enjoyment. The defects of materialism keep us riveted to the world and its pleasures, comforts, and material satisfaction. This does not permit us to think that Divinity is behind all our mental, physical, emotional and intellectual activities. Divinity alone enables us to exist and perform all our functions. Without knowing the Source, whatever we do for our personal enjoyment is bound to create troubles. Sri Ramakrishna says:

As long as there is bhoga (enjoyment), there will be less of yoga. Furthermore, bhoga begets suffering. . . . [A] kite had a fish in his beak; so it was surrounded by a thousand crows. Whichever way it flew with the fish, the crows pursued it crying, "Caw! Caw!" When all of a sudden the fish dropped from its beak, the crows flew after the fish, leaving the kite alone.

The "fish" is the object of enjoyment. The "crows" are worries and anxiety. Worries and anxiety are inevitable with enjoyment. No sooner does one give up enjoyment than one finds peace. (*Gospel*, p. 428)

According to Jung:

Once man is set to pursuit of external things, he is never satisfied, as experience shows, with the mere necessities of life but always strives after more and more, which, true to his prejudices, he always seeks in external things. . . , The inner man raises his claim which cannot be satisfied by any external goods. The externalization leads to an incurable suffering because of one's own nature. . . . It is this which forms the illness of the westerner and he does not rest until he has infected the whole world with his greedy restlessness. The wisdom and mysticism of the East have, therefore, a very great deal to tell us, provided they speak in their own inimitable speech. . . . The life and teachings of Sri Ramana are not only important for the Indians, but also for the western[ers]. Not only do they form a record of great human interest, but also a warning message to a humanity which threatens to lose itself in the chaos of its unconsciousness and lack of self-control. (Quoted from *Prabuddha Bharata*, Oct. 1987, p. 383)

## LASTING JOY OF SPIRITUAL STRENGTH

The lasting joy of spiritual strength displaces impermanent, material enjoyment. The lessons of life and history give us this important insight that no amount of material success will ever give us lasting satisfaction; it will only give us repeated sorrow. Sri Ramakrishna says:

> The bound creatures, entangled in worldliness, will not come to their senses at all. They suffer so much misery and agony, they face so many dangers, and yet they will not wake up.

> The camel loves to eat thorny bushes. The more it eats the thorns, the more blood gushes from its mouth. Still it must eat thorny plants and will never give them up. The man of worldly nature suffers so much sorrow and afflictions, but he forgets it all in a few days and begins his old life over again. Suppose a man has lost his wife or she has turned unfaithful. Lo! He marries again. (*Gospel*, p. 165)

What is the way out? How can we be free? We must come out of materialism's narrow groove and accept the spiritual insight of the great mystics, which is in harmony with nature. However difficult it may be to conquer one's lower nature, it is entirely within everyone's grasp to nurture the soul's power:

> . . . lofty thoughts that ennoble his little day; disdaining the coward terrors of the slave of Fate, to worship at the shrine that his own hands have built; . . . proudly defiant

of the irresistible forces that tolerate, for a moment, his knowledge and his condemnation, to sustain alone, a weary but unyielding Atlas, the world that his own ideals have fashioned despite the trampling march of unconscious power. (Bertrand Russell, "A Free Man's Worship," in *Mysticism and Logic* [London, 1959], pp. 48-9)

We develop by controlling the inner as well as the outer impulses in order to harness the spiritual potentiality lying dormant within us. The whole problem boils down to the prevalent materialistic attitude where we strain every nerve to satisfy the senses by focusing all our energy on the body and the outer world. This is the wrong perspective. It makes us feel defeated and inferior, feelings that generate envy, jealousy, hatred, fear, anger, and insecurity.

In conclusion, Arnold Toynbee's prescient remarks are relevant:

In the present age, the world has been united on the material plane by Western technology. But this Western skill has not only "annihilated distance"; it has armed the peoples of the world with weapons of devastating power at a time when they have been brought to point-blank range of each other without yet having learnt to know and love each other. At this supremely dangerous moment in human history, the only way of salvation for mankind is an Indian way. The Emperor Ashoka's and the Mahatma Gandhi's principle of non-violence and Sri Ramakrishna's testimony to the harmony of religions: here we have the attitude and the spirit that can make it possible for the human race to grow together into a single family—and, in the Atomic Age, this is the only alternative to destroying ourselves. (Arnold Toynbee's forward to Swami

Ghanananda, *Sri Ramakrishna and His Unique Message*
[London, 1970])

We develop our soul-consciousness and acquire "the Indian way" of spiritual knowledge by struggling hard to keep thinking of the Divinity behind the body and the outer world. Dr. Jung was convinced that salvation for the world depends on the salvation of each individual soul that discovers its true inner nature: "It is, unfortunately, only too clear that if the individual is not truly regenerated in spirit, society cannot be either, for society is the sum total of individuals in need of redemption" (C. G. Jung, *The Undiscovered Self* [New York and Toronto: A Mentor Book by The New American Library, 1958], p. 68). A spiritual perspective alone develops our soul-consciousness and makes life meaningful — the gift of religion to humanity.

## UNIVERSAL MESSAGE OF THE ETERNAL PHILOSOPHY

The ideas recommended in this work comprise our humble contribution towards finding a solution to the myraid problems that the world faces today. These have been culled from the eternal principles of Vedanta, whose universal teachings are for the whole world. Swamiji writes:

> The problem of life is becoming deeper and broader every day as the world moves on. The watchword and the essence have been preached in the days of yore when the Vedantic truth was first discovered, the solidarity of life. One atom in this universe cannot move without dragging the whole world along with it. There cannot be any progress without the whole world following in the wake, and it is becoming every day clearer that the solution of

any problem can never be attained on racial, or national, or narrow grounds. Every idea has to become broad till it covers the whole of this world; every aspiration must go on increasing till it has engulfed the whole of humanity, nay, the whole of life with its scope. (*C. W.*, I: 269)

The world needs this broadness of mind and heart. Let us sympathize with others in their suffering and serve them to alleviate their misery; our pain will thus lose its intensity. Helping others, we cure ourselves. Good deeds bring joy and smiles to others and help us forget our ego. Religion asks us to expand ourselves; contraction is irreligious and akin to death.

This humble work contains but a few significant suggestions so as to inculcate a truly spiritual life according to the essential message common to all the major religions. If any one of these is followed sincerely and wholeheartedly, without becoming dogmatic, it will, we are sure, lead to happiness, enlightenment, and peace. We all want to escape the dangers of the global village and continue to enjoy its benefits. We can do this if we practise the eternal ideals embedded within every true religion and transform our lives by developing both our spiritual vision and an enlightened attitude. Any rational person is welcome to receive the wonderful teachings of Vedanta. Whether we are conscious of it or not, they permeate the world, broaden our minds and vision as we practise them, and transform our lives in a world that is searching for the universal spirit of religion.